PRACTICAL ORIGAMI

Tuck, wrap, flatten, layer, gift, decorate.
Turn simple paper into all kinds of useful objects.

VERTICAL.

Contents

Tabletop Decorations

Contents

Decorations for Every Season

Finished origami may look different than the photos due to differences in folds or paper weight.

Basic folds and symbols explained

Here are basic folding techniques and the symbols used in the patterns in this book.

Valley Fold

Marked with a dashed line. Fold so that the dotted line will end up inside.

Valley fold line

Fold in the direction of the arrow

Mountain Fold

Marked with a dot-and-dash line. Fold so that the line will end up outside.

Mountain fold line

Fold under, according to the arrow

Make a Crease

Creases are used as guides for steps that come later on.
Fold according to diagram, then return to previous position.

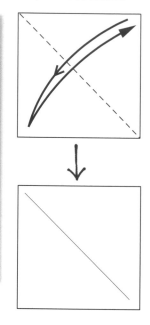

Squash Fold

Insert finger where indicated by the gray arrow. Open according to directional arrow, then flatten into a new fold.

* These are some examples of squash folds. Many variations exist.

Inside Reverse Fold

Create diagonal mountain fold, then tuck top point in between sides.

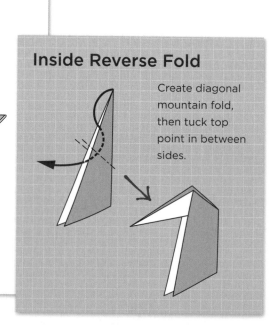

Materials, tools, tips and tricks

Paper and folding techniques that will create origami sturdy enough to be functional, with a pattern or design you'll enjoy seeing time and again.

Create Strong Creases

Paper that's sturdy and resilient enough for practical goods is also a little tough to fold. Using the tools listed will aid in creating strong, clean creases that will support the final shape.

Tools

Cutting Board	For use under the origami paper.
Metal Ruler	Won't get cut up when using a utility knife
X-Acto (Utility) Knifer	When cutting paper down to a smaller size, a utility knife combined with a ruler makes cleaner lines than scissors.
Craft Spatula	Used when creating creases. A stylus or empty ball point pen will also work.
Pencil	Use to lightly draw folding patterns

1 Lightly draw folding pattern on paper. Crease along lines with spatula.

2 This allows you to fold the paper along the creases more easily. Fold each crease once before putting whole origami together.

Skewers for Clean Corners

Tools

Skewers allow you to make sharp corners that won't collapse. Use the skewer point to hold the corner in place when you fold. This is especially useful for designs with some height.

Bamboo Skewer	An awl or toothpick will also work.
Glue	Useful for preserving the origami's final shape.

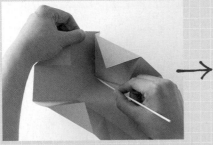

1 Fold along creases while holding down corner with the skewer.

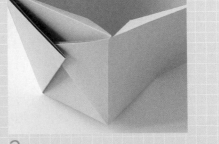

2 Nice, sharp corners! If the folds won't stay in place, use glue.

Gorgeous Everyday Containers

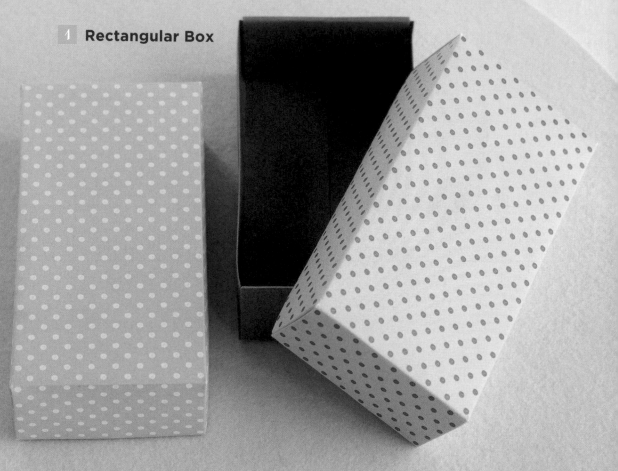

1 Rectangular Box

Adorable and durable for all kinds of things!

Use either regular or Japanese washi paper with a nice pattern and turn it into a nifty box. For the base, use paper in a solid color that matches the patterned paper for an elegant look.

Instructions ······· **20**

A slender gift box for their favorite sweets.

2 | **Sweets Box**

Put macarons or chocolate truffles into
this slim gift box. Line it with delicately
patterned paper to bring it to the next level.

Instructions ⋯⋯ 22

A colorful package makes a homemade
pound cake look all the more enticing. I made
this paper by copying a napkin with stripes.

Instructions ······ **24**

3 **Pound Cake Box**

The perfect choice for pot lucks or parties!

4

Add details like buttons to make it extra chic.

5

Open Box

This box, with the double-opening top, is a more elegant take on the classic box. Try adding ribbons or buttons to dress it up.

Instructions ⋯⋯ **25**

6 **Cookie Box**

This cute box opens up
like a blossom.

Just crease and fold! Wrap the cookies in
tissue paper and leave the edges outside,
creating a bloom of paper.

Instructions ⋯⋯ **26**

A piece of paper turns
into a proper gift bag.

7　Gift Bag

The gussets on the sides of this
bag make it very convenient for
a wide variety of gifts. Paper
printed with the same pattern as
the handkerchief inside doubles
the surprise!

Instructions ⋯⋯ **27**

Clever boxes for snack-centric parties.

8 **Deli Box**

These handy little boxes make for easy snacking and add a touch of fun to party foods. Line with plastic wrap or foil for heavier cuisine.

Instructions ·······**29**

10 Cutlery Case

A recyclable, eye-pleasing solution for homemade lunches. Try making with all kinds of patterned paper!

Instructions ······ **28**

9 Lunch Box

Easy to take to the park or on a hike!

Boxes of all sizes to keep your desk or
dresser organized.

11 **Square Box**

You can resize the pattern according to your
needs, making this an exceptionally useful piece.
Try using different colors for different items.

Instructions ······**30**

16

Here are two versions of this cube-shaped drawer. I made printed copies of the contents for a whimsical take on organization.

Instructions ⋯⋯ 32

12 **Small Drawer**

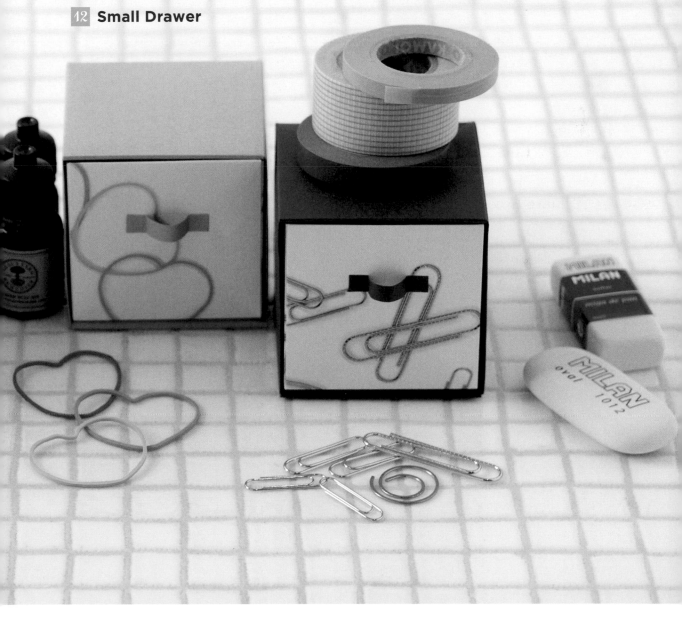

Pop art or classical?

13 **Two-Tone Box**

Using contrasting papers gives you an array
of decorative motifs. This one's especially
suited for use as gift wrapping.

Instructions ⸱⸱⸱⸱⸱⸱ **34**

Make your own bag with your favorite pattern.

14 Bag with Handles

Try turning a nice piece of wrapping paper into a bag. This is very simple to make, so it's wide open for interpretation.

Instructions 36

1 Rectangular Box (photo pg 8)

Paper size : Base 28 x 28 cm Lid 29 x 29 cm

Finished size : 7 x 14 x 3.5 cm (interior capacity)

Note : The lid is larger than the base, but both are folded the same way.

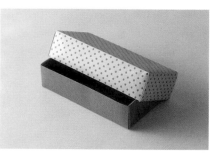

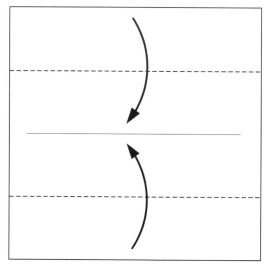

1 Lightly mark the center. Fold the top and bottom edges to the center.

2 Fold top and bottom edges to the center.

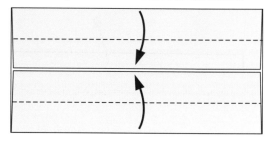

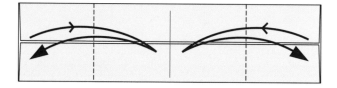

3 Lightly mark center, then fold right and left edges to the center, then unfold.

4 Fold left and right edges to the left and right creases, then unfold.

5 Crease diagonally by folding and unfolding the bottom left and right corners.

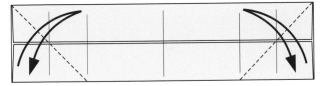

6 Repeat with top left and right corners.

Resizing this design:

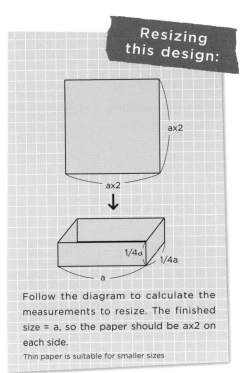

Follow the diagram to calculate the measurements to resize. The finished size = a, so the paper should be ax2 on each side.

Thin paper is suitable for smaller sizes

7 Fold along dotted lines, then open up middle section.

8 Fold and tuck in right and left ends to complete shape.

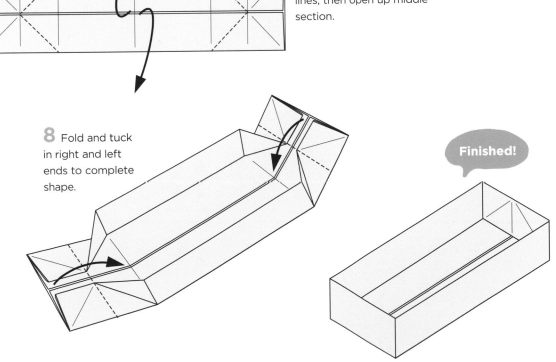

Finished!

21

2 **Sweets Box** (photo pg 9)

Paper size : Large 45 x 45 cm   Small 30 x 30 cm

Finished size : Large 5.8 x 33.5 x 5.8 cm

Small 3.8 x 22.5 x 3.8 cm

Note : Use sturdy, resilient paper that's not too thick.

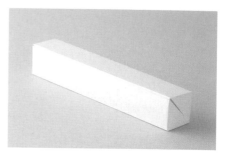

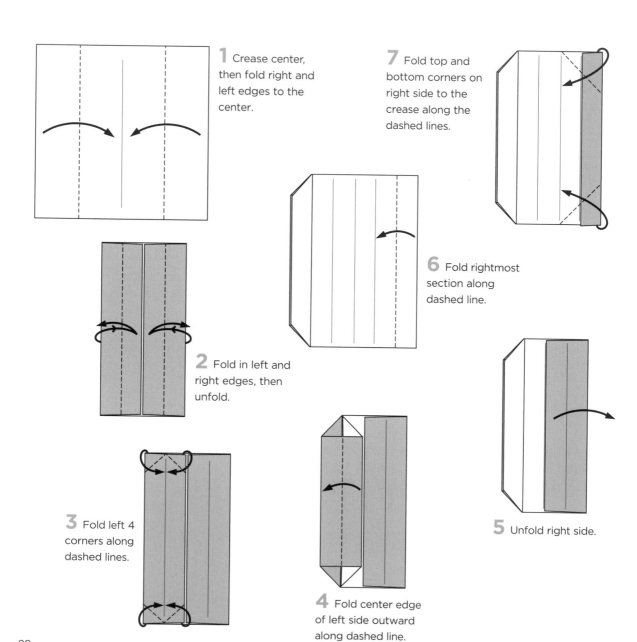

1 Crease center, then fold right and left edges to the center.

2 Fold in left and right edges, then unfold.

3 Fold left 4 corners along dashed lines.

4 Fold center edge of left side outward along dashed line.

5 Unfold right side.

6 Fold rightmost section along dashed line.

7 Fold top and bottom corners on right side to the crease along the dashed lines.

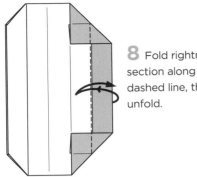

8 Fold rightmost section along dashed line, then unfold.

Finished!

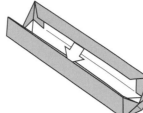

14 Insert flap from top into opening on bottom to hold in place.

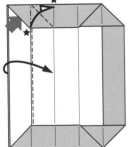

9 Fold along dashed lines (between the red circles).

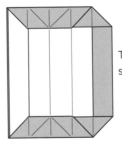

13 Following creases made in steps 10 through 12, refold to create box.

This is how it should look.

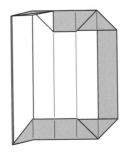

10 Squash fold where indicated by arrow. Align points (marked by stars) and crease base, creating a corner.

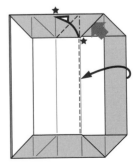

12 Repeat steps 10 and 11 on the right side, squash folding and aligning points (marked by stars). Unfold.

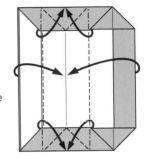

11 This is how it should look. Repeat with lower left corner, then flatten both corners (returning to step 10).

3 Pound Cake Box (photo pg 10)

Paper size : Large 48 x 42 cm   Small 33 x 28 cm

Finished size : Large 10 x 22 x 8 cm
Small 7 x 14 x 5 cm

Note : Line bottom with heavy paper to reinforce. If the box is too big for the cake, line with packing materials to keep it from moving.

See page 33 for instructions on resizing patterns.

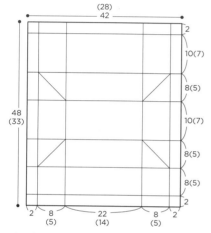

(Numbers in parentheses are for the small size)

1 Lightly draw lines on the back according to the diagram and use a craft spatula to crease.

2 Fold along dashed lines in the direction of the arrows in order listed.

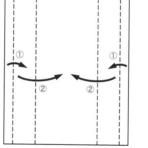

3 Valley fold on top; mountain fold on the bottom.

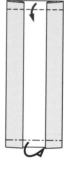

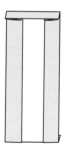

This is how it should look.

4 Unfold (except for far left and right sections). Fold along dashed lines and crease well, then unfold.

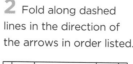

5 Mountain fold along dot-and-dash lines in the direction of the arrows.

Use a skewer or toothpick to keep the corner from collapsing when you fold into place.

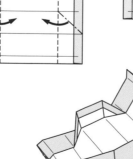

This is how it should look.

Finished!

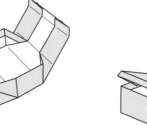

4 5 Open Box (photo pg 11)

Paper size : Large 52 x 34 cm Small 32 x 22 cm

Finished size : Large 14 x 14 x 9 cm
Small 10 x 10 x 5 cm

Note : Use paper with some resilience to it.
Use tracing paper for 5. The folding pattern
is basically the same as the Pound Cake Box.

See page 33 for instructions on resizing patterns.

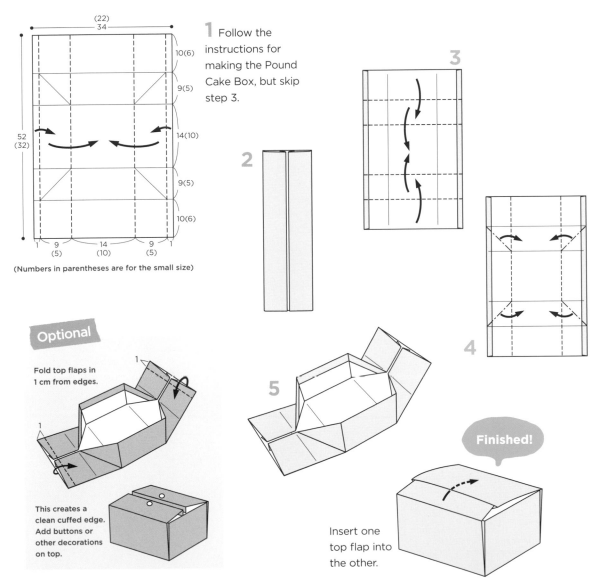

1 Follow the instructions for making the Pound Cake Box, but skip step 3.

(Numbers in parentheses are for the small size)

Optional

Fold top flaps in 1 cm from edges.

This creates a clean cuffed edge. Add buttons or other decorations on top.

Finished!

Insert one top flap into the other.

25

6 Cookie Box (photo pg 12)

Paper size : Large 44 x 44 cm   Small 28 x 28 cm
Finished size : Large 15.5 x 15.5 x 8.5 cm
   Small 10 x 10 x 5.5 cm
Note : Use thick paper and a craft spatula to create creases. The finished product shows both sides of the paper, so keep that in mind when choosing which paper to use.

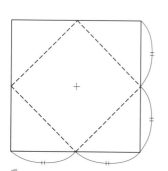

1 Mark the center, then use a spatula to crease along the dashed lines.

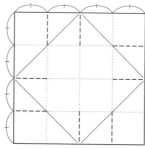

2 Crease along dashed lines. (The gray dotted lines are there as guides only; do not crease.)

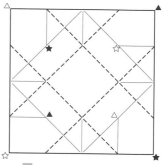

3 Crease along dashed lines. Alternatively, match points marked with matching symbols, fold to crease, unfold.

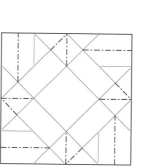

4 Crease along dot-and-dash lines, then mountain fold.

5 After folding along each line, fold each section together in order, counter-clockwise.

Fold each pleat over the previous one.

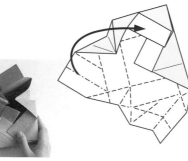

Tuck last pleat on left underneath the first.

Finished!

7 Gift Bag (photo pg 13)

Paper size : Large 40 x 40 cm   Small 30 x 30 cm

Finished size : Large 17 x 17 cm (gusset: 5 cm)
Small 13 x 13 cm (gusset: 4 cm)

Note : If using the bag for something heavy, use durable paper and/or reinforce the folds with glue or finishing spray.

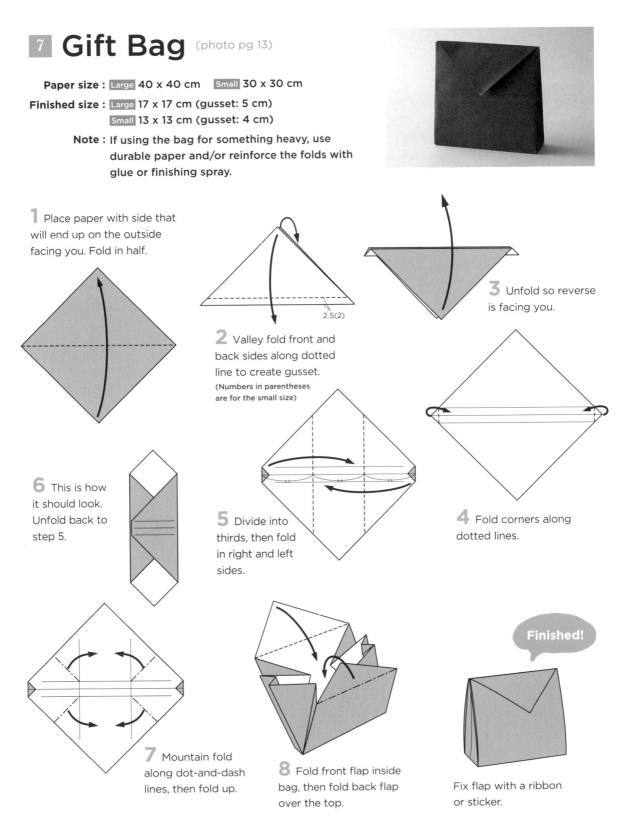

1 Place paper with side that will end up on the outside facing you. Fold in half.

2 Valley fold front and back sides along dotted line to create gusset.
(Numbers in parentheses are for the small size)

2.5(2)

3 Unfold so reverse is facing you.

4 Fold corners along dotted lines.

5 Divide into thirds, then fold in right and left sides.

6 This is how it should look. Unfold back to step 5.

7 Mountain fold along dot-and-dash lines, then fold up.

8 Fold front flap inside bag, then fold back flap over the top.

Finished!

Fix flap with a ribbon or sticker.

27

9 Lunch Box (photo pg 15)

Paper size : 60 x 44 cm

Finished size : 15 x 20 x 6 cm

Note : Since the back of the lid will be visible once the box is opened, paste two sheets of paper together face-out to reinforce and make it more presentable.

See page 33 for instructions on resizing patterns.

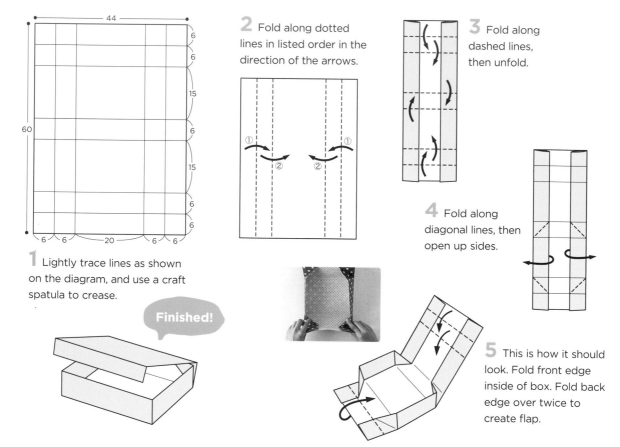

1 Lightly trace lines as shown on the diagram, and use a craft spatula to crease.

2 Fold along dotted lines in listed order in the direction of the arrows.

3 Fold along dashed lines, then unfold.

4 Fold along diagonal lines, then open up sides.

5 This is how it should look. Fold front edge inside of box. Fold back edge over twice to create flap.

Finished!

---

10 Cutlery Case (photo pg 15)

Paper size : 24 x 24 cm

Finished size : 17 x 9 cm

Note : Either paste two pieces of paper with face side out or use double-sided paper.

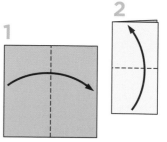

1 Fold in half widthwise, then half again lengthwise.

2

8 Deli Box (photo pg 14)

Paper size : Large Base 36 x 36 cm, Lid 19 x 19 cm
Medium Base 30 x 30 cm, Lid 17 x 17 cm
Small Base 21 x 21 cm, Lid 12.5 x 12.5 cm

Finished size : Large 19 x 19 x 20.5 cm
Medium 11 x 11 x 12 cm
Small 8 x 8 x 8.5 cm

Note : These work best with heavy craft paper or even card stock. Crease well before folding up. Make sure the corners stay put to keep box from collapsing.

1 On the back of the paper, lightly trace lines according to the diagram and crease with a spatula. Make mountain (dot-and-dash) and valley (dash) folds accordingly.

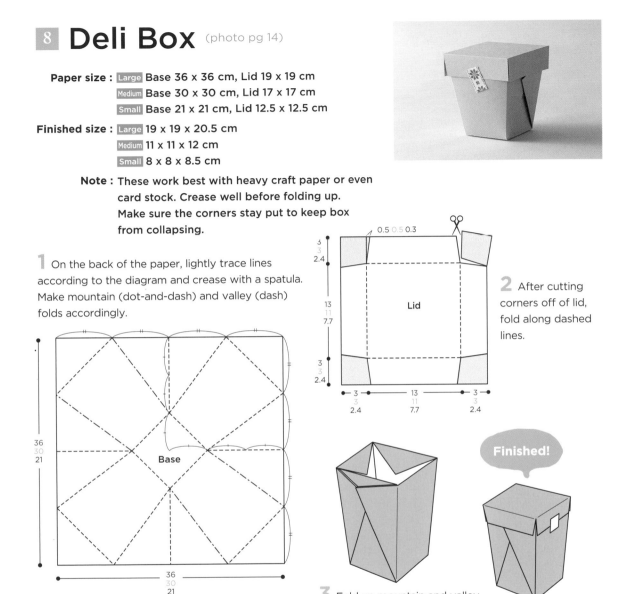

Base

36
30
21

36
30
21

Red numbers are for large,
blue for medium, **and black for small.**

Lid

0.5 0.5 0.3

5
3
2.4

13
11
7.7

3
3
2.4

3
3
2.4

13
11
7.7

3
3
2.4

2 After cutting corners off of lid, fold along dashed lines.

3 Fold up mountain and valley folds.

Finished!

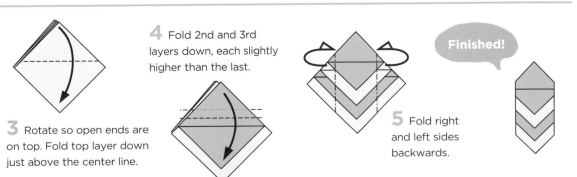

3 Rotate so open ends are on top. Fold top layer down just above the center line.

4 Fold 2nd and 3rd layers down, each slightly higher than the last.

5 Fold right and left sides backwards.

Finished!

29

11 Square Box (photo pg 16)

Paper size : `Large` Base 29.5 x 29.5 cm, Lid 23 x 23 cm
`Medium` Base 22.5 x 22.5 cm, Lid 17 x 17 cm
`Small` Base 17 x 17 cm, Lid 13 x 13 cm

Finished size : `Large` 10.5 x 10.5 x 5 cm (interior)
`Medium` 8 x 8 x 4 cm (interior)
`Small` 6 x 6 x 3 cm (interior)

Note : The size and proportions of the folds differ between the base and the lid but both are made using the same folding process.

See page 33 for instructions on resizing patterns.

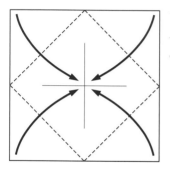

1 Mark the center, then fold in all 4 corners.

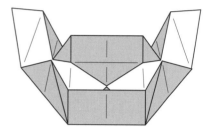

This is how it should look.

2 Fold top and bottom edges to the center.

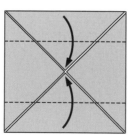

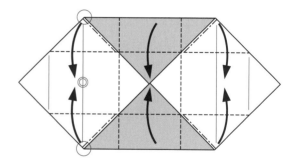

5 Unfold according to diagram. Fold up in the direction of the arrows, so the points marked by circles meet in the middle (repeat on right).

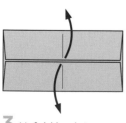

3 Unfold back to beginning of step 2.

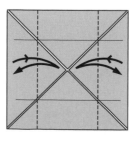

4 Fold right and left edges to the center, then unfold.

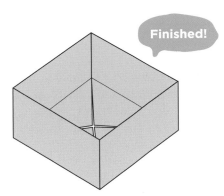

6 Fold left and right flaps inside so the triangular parts line the bottom.

Finished!

Fold the Lid:

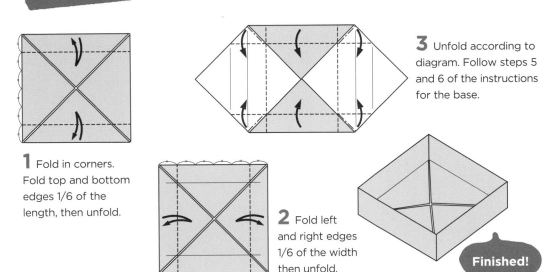

1 Fold in corners. Fold top and bottom edges 1/6 of the length, then unfold.

2 Fold left and right edges 1/6 of the width then unfold.

3 Unfold according to diagram. Follow steps 5 and 6 of the instructions for the base.

Finished!

When working with striped paper:

When using striped or checked paper, the stripe direction will change once it's folded.

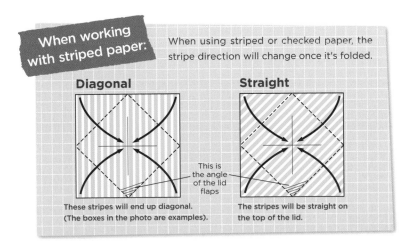

Diagonal

This is the angle of the lid flaps

These stripes will end up diagonal. (The boxes in the photo are examples).

Straight

The stripes will be straight on the top of the lid.

Here are all three sizes.

12 Small Drawer (photo pg 17)

Paper size : Case 29 x 29 cm   Drawer 28 x 28 cm

Finished size : Drawer 6.5 x 6.5 x 6.5 cm (interior)

Note : If you're planning on using this for heavy items, be sure to use sturdy craft paper or reinforce the folds with glue or spray.

See page 33 for instructions on resizing patterns.

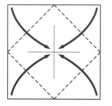

1 Mark center, then fold in the 4 corners.

2 Divide into thirds lengthwise and fold in top and bottom edges, then unfold.

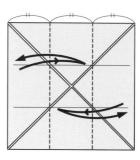

3 Divide into thirds widthwise and fold left and right edges, then unfold.

4 Unfold according to diagram. Mountain fold along dot-and-dashed lines. Match up points marked with circles (same on left and right sides).

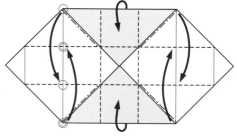

5 Fold in left and right flaps so triangular parts lie on the bottom.

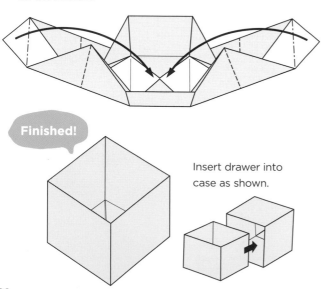

Finished!

Insert drawer into case as shown.

You can also make a cube with a lid!

You can use the lid for the Square Box (page 30) with this drawer. Just use paper that's 15.5 x 15.5 cm.

How to Resize Patterns

Make boxes in any size to suit your needs. Use these diagrams to calculate the size of the paper needed to create the right size.

*These are based on standard paper. Thicker paper will allow for slightly less interior volume.

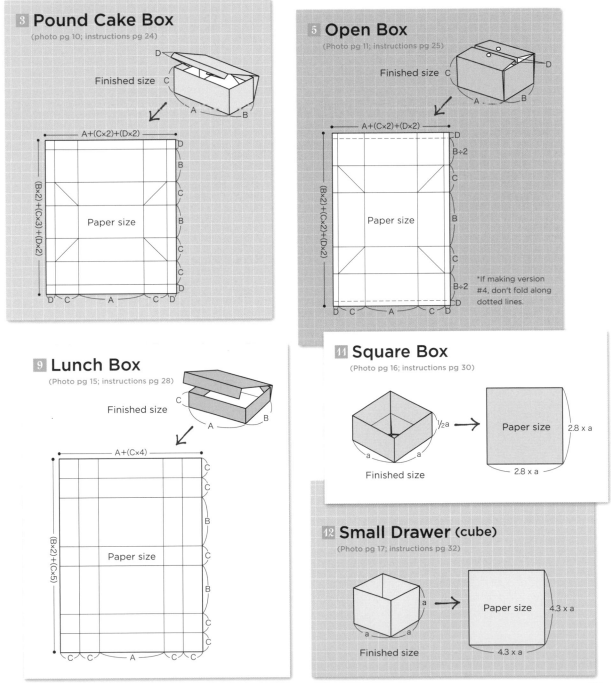

3 Pound Cake Box
(photo pg 10; instructions pg 24)

Finished size

Paper size

A+(C×2)+(D×2)

(B×2)+(C×3)+(D×2)

5 Open Box
(Photo pg 11; instructions pg 25)

Finished size

Paper size

A+(C×2)+(D×2)

(B×2)+(C×2)+(D×2)

B÷2

B÷2

*If making version #4, don't fold along dotted lines.

9 Lunch Box
(Photo pg 15; instructions pg 28)

Finished size

Paper size

A+(C×4)

(B×2)+(C×5)

11 Square Box
(Photo pg 16; instructions pg 30)

Finished size

Paper size

2.8 x a

2.8 x a

½a

12 Small Drawer (cube)
(Photo pg 17; instructions pg 32)

Finished size

Paper size

4.3 x a

4.3 x a

43 Two-Tone Box (photo pg 18)

Paper size : Lid Large **21 x 30 cm (4 sheets)**
Small **18 x 26 cm (4 sheets)**

Base Large **31 x 31 cm** Small **27.5 x 27.5 cm**

Finished size : Large **7.5 x 7.5 x 7.5 cm (interior)**
Small **6.6 x 6.6 x 6.6 cm (interior)**

Note : Use 2 sheets of each color. This is easier to make with paper that's not too thick. Make the base by following the instructions on page 32 for the Small Drawer.

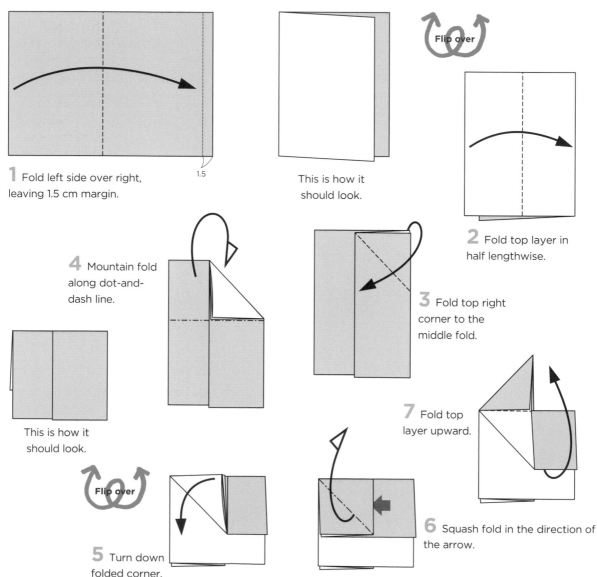

1 Fold left side over right, leaving 1.5 cm margin.

1.5

This is how it should look.

2 Fold top layer in half lengthwise.

3 Fold top right corner to the middle fold.

4 Mountain fold along dot-and-dash line.

This is how it should look.

Flip over

5 Turn down folded corner.

6 Squash fold in the direction of the arrow.

7 Fold top layer upward.

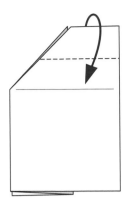

8 Fold top edge of top section to the crease.

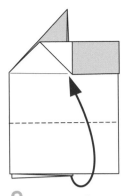

9 Fold entire bottom section so edges meet the crease.

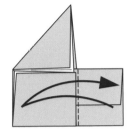

10 Fold top section down and tuck under bottom flap.

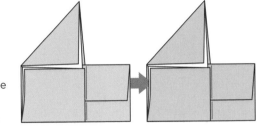

12 Insert right tab from one piece into the slot of contrasting piece.

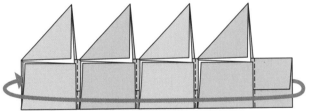

11 Fold right section over left, then unfold. Repeat from step 1 with remaining sheets of paper.

13 Connect all four pieces, alternating colors. Insert tab from fourth piece into slot of first piece.

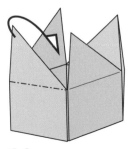

14 Fold down each triangular flap so it overlaps the previous flap.

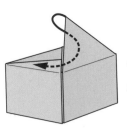

15 Tuck last flap under first flap.

Finished!

14 Bag with Handles (photo pg 19)

Paper size : Large 63 x 63 cm Small 40 x 40 cm
Finished size : Large 18 x 22 cm (Gusset: 4 to 8 cm)
  Small 11.5 x 14 cm (Gusset: 3 to 6 cm)
Note : If the bag will be used for heavy objects, use thick paper and reinforce folds and handle bases with glue or finishing spray.

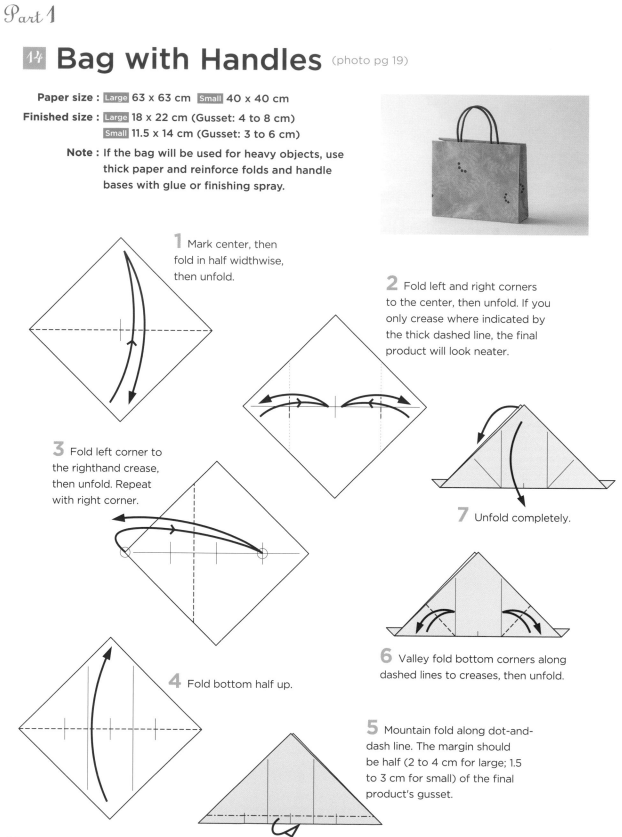

1 Mark center, then fold in half widthwise, then unfold.

2 Fold left and right corners to the center, then unfold. If you only crease where indicated by the thick dashed line, the final product will look neater.

3 Fold left corner to the righthand crease, then unfold. Repeat with right corner.

7 Unfold completely.

4 Fold bottom half up.

6 Valley fold bottom corners along dashed lines to creases, then unfold.

5 Mountain fold along dot-and-dash line. The margin should be half (2 to 4 cm for large; 1.5 to 3 cm for small) of the final product's gusset.

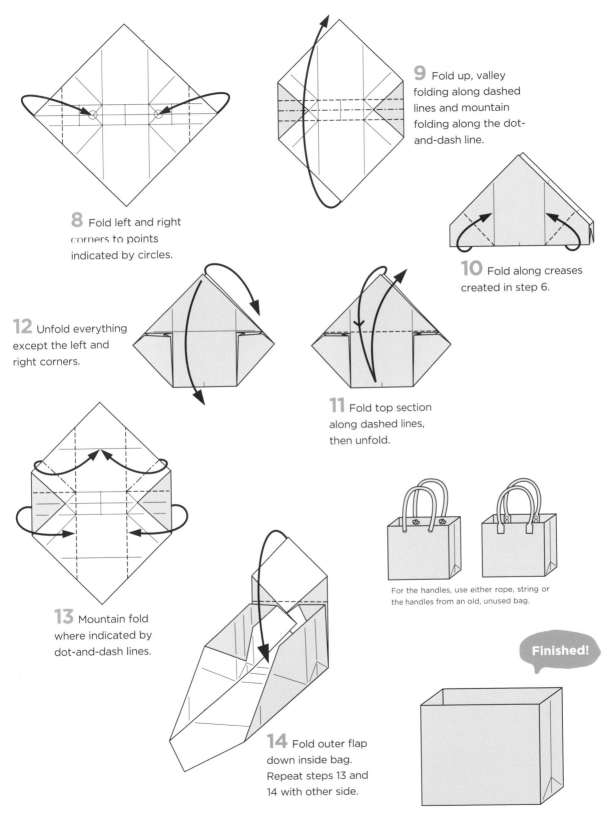

8 Fold left and right corners to points indicated by circles.

9 Fold up, valley folding along dashed lines and mountain folding along the dot-and-dash line.

10 Fold along creases created in step 6.

11 Fold top section along dashed lines, then unfold.

12 Unfold everything except the left and right corners.

13 Mountain fold where indicated by dot-and-dash lines.

14 Fold outer flap down inside bag. Repeat steps 13 and 14 with other side.

For the handles, use either rope, string or the handles from an old, unused bag.

Finished!

Part 2
Tabletop Decorations

Use patterns that make the cuisine look even more appetizing.

15 Chopsticks Envelope

Japanese-style chopsticks wrappers. Try making them with all kinds of fun papers. These will dress up your dinner table no matter what's on the menu.

Instructions ······ **50**

Add pop art to parties or special events.

Combine papers with funky patterns to create these pop art envelopes. These will make any event instantly memorable.

Instructions ······ 51

16 **Pop Chopsticks Envelope**

Decorate your table with these cute and chic handmade objects.

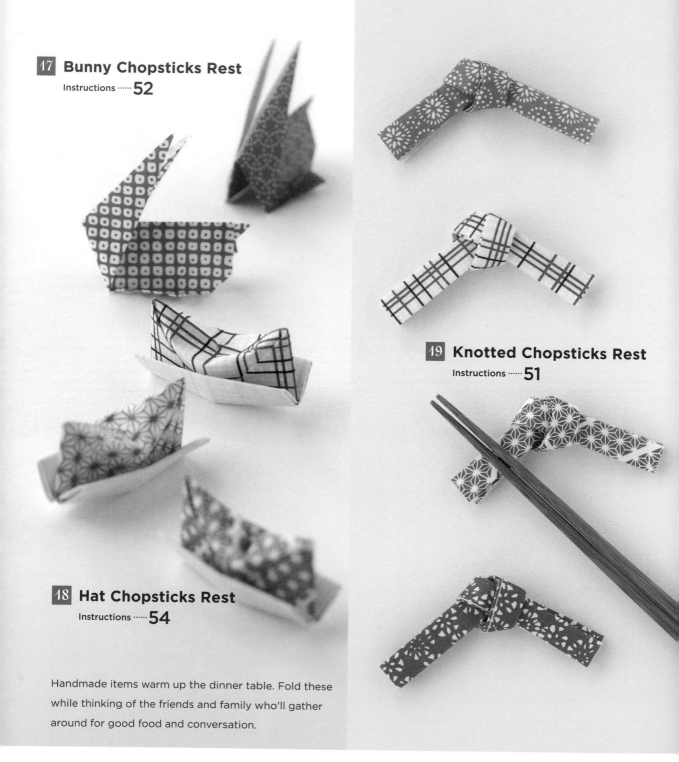

17 **Bunny Chopsticks Rest**

Instructions **52**

19 **Knotted Chopsticks Rest**

Instructions **51**

18 **Hat Chopsticks Rest**

Instructions **54**

Handmade items warm up the dinner table. Fold these while thinking of the friends and family who'll gather around for good food and conversation.

Make these delicate trays out of your favorite craft paper.

20 Boat Tray

If someone brings you snacks as a souvenir, try turning the wrapping paper into a tray to serve the snacks on to show your gratitude. They're sure to be impressed!

Instructions ⋯⋯ **56**

Add a touch of delicacy to your tea time.

23 Serving Paper

24 Crane Serving Paper

25 Toothpick Holder

Make these origami with an eye towards hospitality. Use subtle colors and patterns to better show off the treats they hold.

Memorize these patterns to keep herbs,
spices and powders neatly organized.

26 Herb Pouch
Instructions ······ **64**

Use these charming herb pouches
to organize your own spice drawer
or when sharing with others.
Pretty yet functional, they make
homemade cuisine all the more
appealing.

Triangle Pouch

Instructions ⋯⋯ **65**

29 Candy Dish

A stylish upgrade to
the typical candy dish.

Your typical hard candies can undergo a makeover with these
dishes. Keep these handy for when friends and family stop by and
they'll be empty in no time. They're surprisingly simple to make.

Instructions ······ **66**

These open top boxes make their sweet contents impossible to resist!

30 Candy Box

The back of the paper provides a nice accent for these candy boxes. Try making these in a variety of sizes.

Instructions **68**

Celebrations shared with loved ones,
with handmade wedding decorations

33 **Card Stand**
Instructions ┄┄┄ **73**

32 **Heart Napkin Ring**
Instructions ┄┄┄ **72**

31 **Cutlery Rest**
Instructions ┄┄┄ **70**

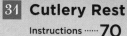

Welcome

34 Photo Frame
Instructions ······ **75**

Use these decorations for an "at home" atmosphere at a wedding. Fold each one with loving thoughts to celebrate the happy couple.

15 Chopsticks Envelope (photo pg 38)

Paper size : 15 x 15 cm

Finished size : 13 x 3.7 cm

Note : The folded-back edge down the center gives it a nice accent. Try making these with paper with a pattern on one side and a plain reverse.

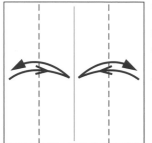

1 Fold left and right edges to the center, then unfold. Repeat to crease thoroughly.

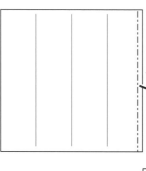

2 Mountain fold right side, 0.4 cm from edge.

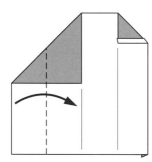

5 Fold left edge to the center.

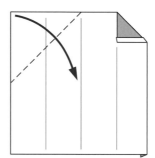

4 Diagonally fold top left corner to the center line.

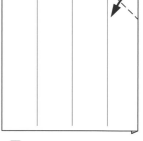

3 Diagonally fold top right corner to right-hand crease.

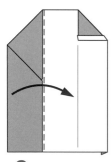

6 Fold left edge to right-hand crease.

7 Fold right edge along crease.

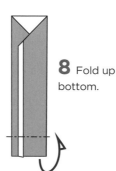

8 Fold up bottom.

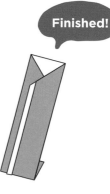

Finished!

16 Pop Chopsticks Envelope (photo pg 39)

Paper size : `Envelope` 18 x 12 cm `Insert` 18 x 4 cm

Finished size : 18 x 4 cm

> **Note :** This is a simple trifold with an insert in a contrasting color.

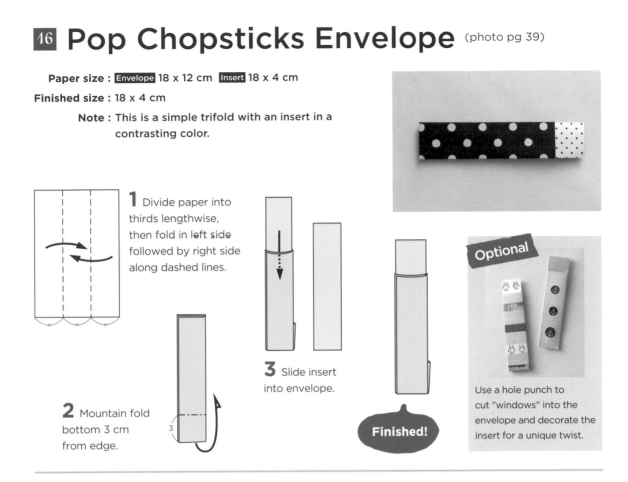

1 Divide paper into thirds lengthwise, then fold in left side followed by right side along dashed lines.

2 Mountain fold bottom 3 cm from edge.

3 Slide insert into envelope.

Finished!

Optional

Use a hole punch to cut "windows" into the envelope and decorate the insert for a unique twist.

19 Knotted Chopsticks Rest (photo pg 40)

Paper size : 6 x 15 cm

Finished size : 3.5 x 7.5 cm

> **Note :** Use flexible and resilient *washi* paper.

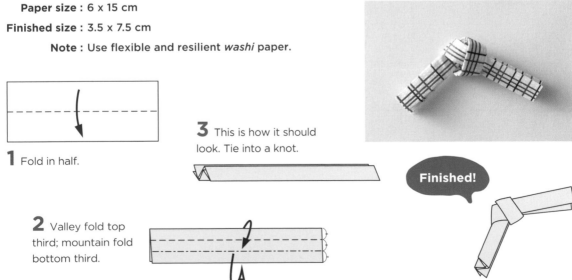

1 Fold in half.

2 Valley fold top third; mountain fold bottom third.

3 This is how it should look. Tie into a knot.

Finished!

17 Bunny Chopsticks Rest <small>(photo pg 40)</small>

Paper size : 7.5 x 7.5 cm

Finished size : 3 x 5 x 4.5 cm

Note : Kids will love this version of a chopsticks rest. Use paper that's sturdy enough to hold the shape.

1 Fold in half to crease, then unfold.

Flip over

This is how it should look.

2 Fold top and bottom left-hand edges to the center crease.

4 Fold tip of triangle on right side along dashed lines, so the tip extends past the edge.

3 Fold right corner along dashed line.

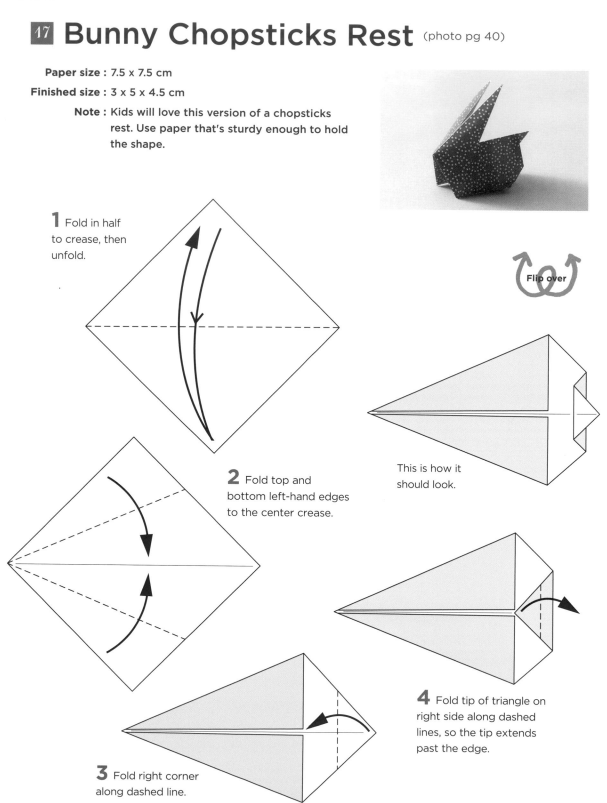

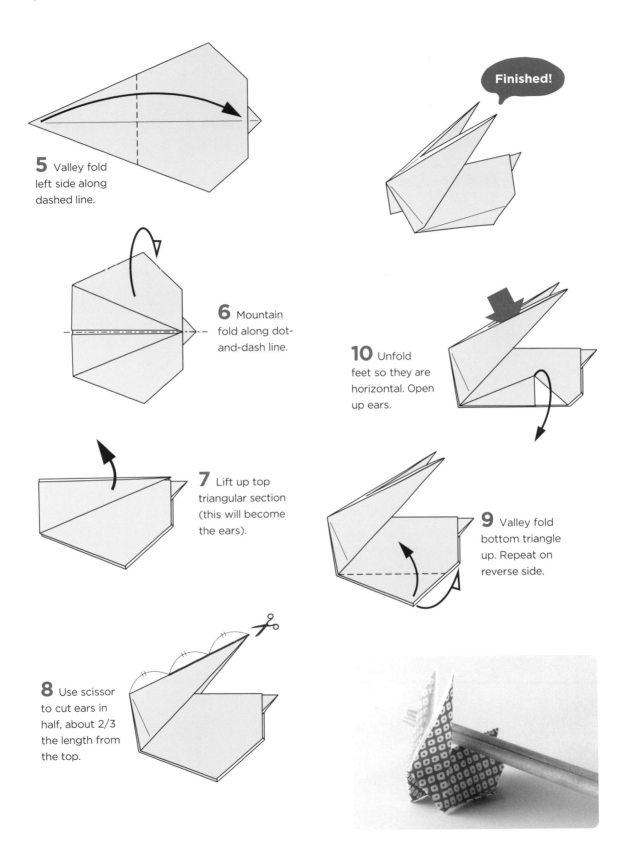

5 Valley fold left side along dashed line.

6 Mountain fold along dot-and-dash line.

7 Lift up top triangular section (this will become the ears).

8 Use scissor to cut ears in half, about 2/3 the length from the top.

9 Valley fold bottom triangle up. Repeat on reverse side.

10 Unfold feet so they are horizontal. Open up ears.

Finished!

18 Hat Chopsticks Rest (photo pg 40)

Paper size : 10 x 10 cm

Finished size : 2 x 5 x 2.5 cm

Note : This is a smaller version of the traditional "hat" origami. If you use paper that's large enough you could actually wear it as a hat!

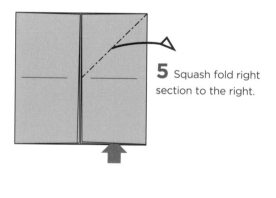

1 Fold in half widthwise.

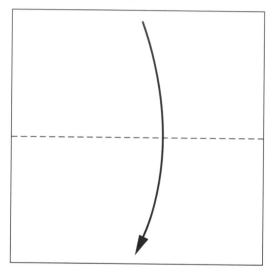

2 Fold in half lengthwise, then unfold.

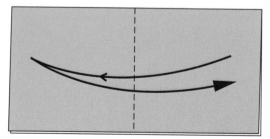

3 Fold in left and right edges so they meet in the center.

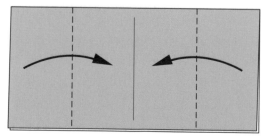

This is how it should look.

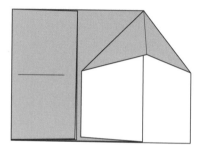

5 Squash fold right section to the right.

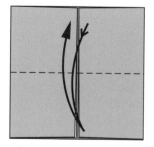

4 Fold in half widthwise, then unfold.

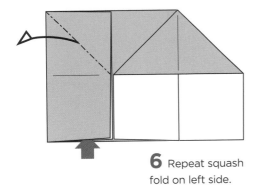

6 Repeat squash fold on left side.

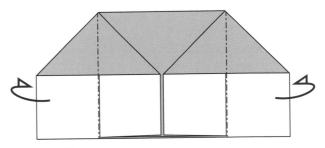

7 Fold left and right sections backwards along dot-and-dash lines.

8 Fold up top layer only along dashed line.

9 Fold same section again, along dashed line.

10 Repeat steps 8 and 9 on reverse side.

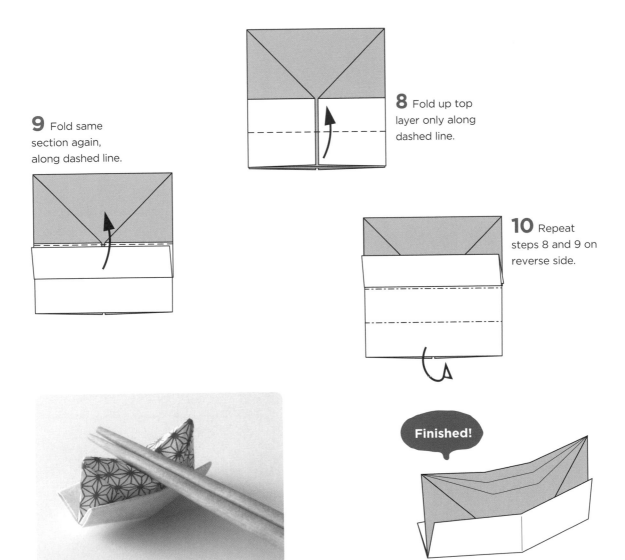

Finished!

20 Boat Tray (photo pg 41)

Paper size : 21 x 21 cm

Finished size : 11.5 x 18.5 x 2.5 cm

Note : Opening up the left and right sides before folding back the top and bottom edges will make it look neater.

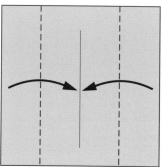

1 Lay paper with printed side facing you. Fold in half lengthwise. Fold in left and right edges so they meet in the center.

2 Fold left and right edges along dashed lines, then unfold.

3 Diagonally fold all 8 corners along dashed lines as shown in the diagram.

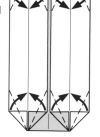

4 Diagonally fold all 8 newly-formed corners along dashed lines.

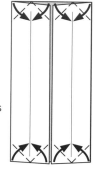

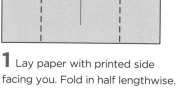

6 Pull out folds on left and right sides.

5 Fold center-right and center-left sections outward.

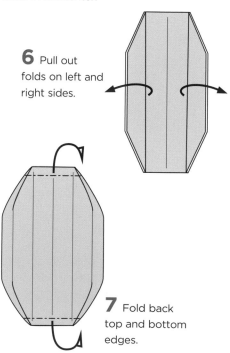

7 Fold back top and bottom edges.

Finished!

24 Crane Serving Papers (photo pg 43)

Paper size : 26 x 23 cm

Finished size : 15 x 26 cm

> **Note :** Serving papers are used in lieu of dishes. Try using them for candies or dried fruit.

1 Lay paper portrait-style. Fold lower right corner along dashed line.

2 Fold bottom corner along dashed line. The corner should extend past the edge of the paper.

3 Mountain fold along dot-and-dash line.

This is how it should look.

This is how it should look.

4 Unfold back to step 2, then mountain and valley fold along lines in the direction of the arrow.

5 Outside reverse fold point to create crane's head.

Finished!

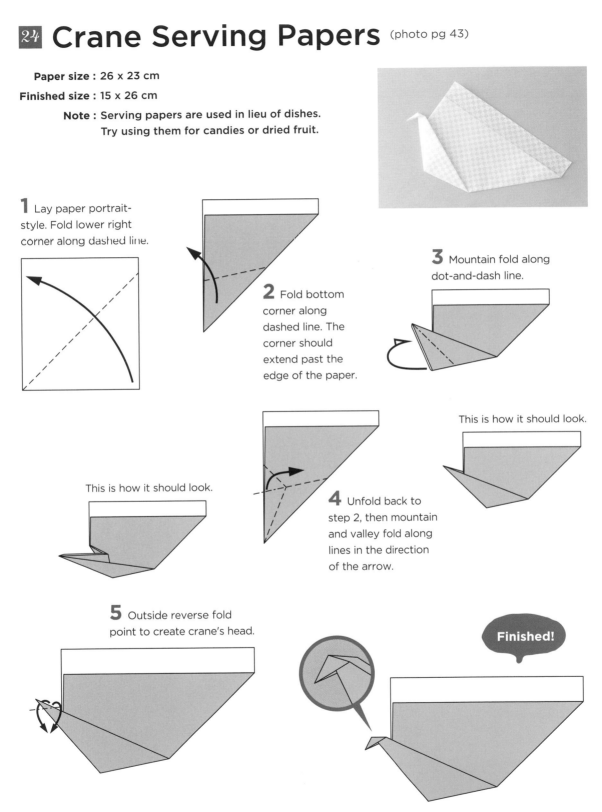

21 Crane Chopsticks Envelope (photo pg 42)

Paper size : 15 x 15 cm

Finished size : 14.5 x 7.5 cm

Note : An elegant take on the humble chopsticks envelope with a crane in the center. Use paper that is a presentable color on both sides.

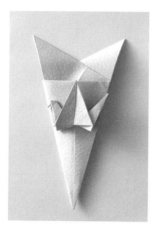

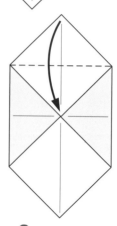

1 Fold top and bottom corners together, then unfold. Repeat with left and right corners. Fold in left and right corners so they meet in the center.

2 Fold top corner to the center.

3 Fold top right and left corners to the center.

4 Unfold back to step 2.

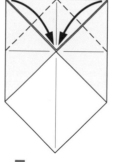

This is how it should look.

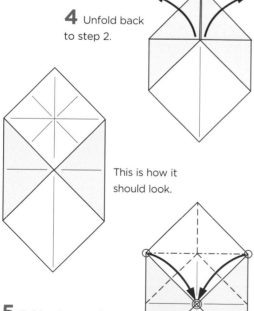

5 Fold points marked with circles to the center (double circle). Valley fold along dashed lines; mountain fold along dot-and-dash lines.

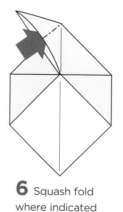

6 Squash fold where indicated by arrow.

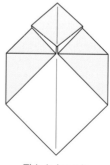

This is how it should look.

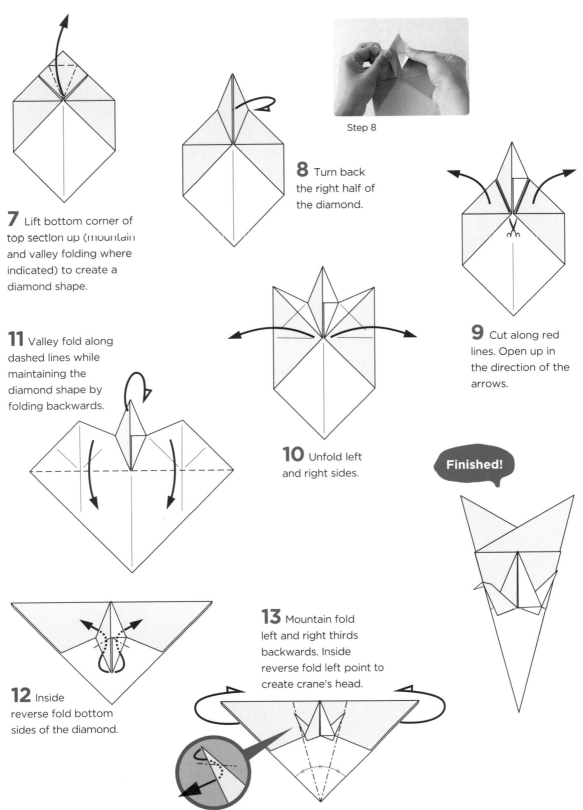

7 Lift bottom corner of top section up (mountain and valley folding where indicated) to create a diamond shape.

8 Turn back the right half of the diamond.

Step 8

9 Cut along red lines. Open up in the direction of the arrows.

10 Unfold left and right sides.

11 Valley fold along dashed lines while maintaining the diamond shape by folding backwards.

Finished!

12 Inside reverse fold bottom sides of the diamond.

13 Mountain fold left and right thirds backwards. Inside reverse fold left point to create crane's head.

59

22 Cherry Blossom Dish (photo pg 42)

Paper size : 8 x 16 cm (5 sheets)

Finished size : 17 x 2 cm

Note : Make five petals then piece them together. Feel free to use the petals themselves as individual dishes.

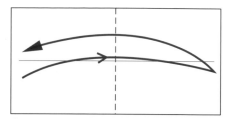

1 Fold in half, then unfold.

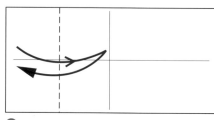

2 Fold left edge to the center, then unfold.

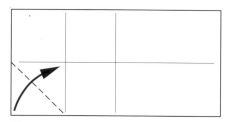

3 Diagonally fold bottom left corner along dashed line.

4 Fold in half widthwise.

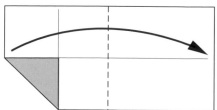

8 Diagonally fold top left corner.

This is how it should look.

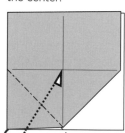

7 Mountain fold top layer only along dot-and-dash line, tucking right edge inside.

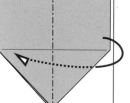

6 Inside reverse fold bottom left corner to the center.

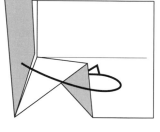

5 Fold bottom left corner along dashed line, then unfold.

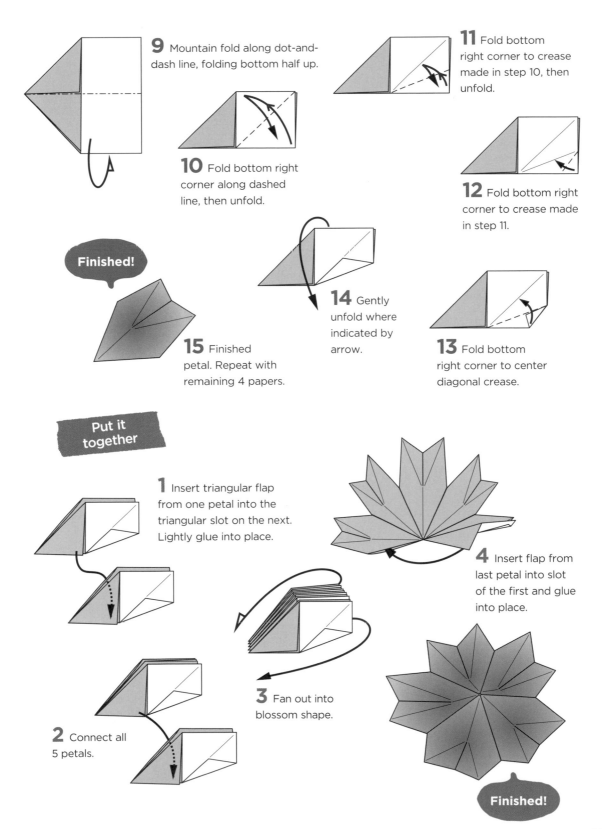

9 Mountain fold along dot-and-dash line, folding bottom half up.

10 Fold bottom right corner along dashed line, then unfold.

11 Fold bottom right corner to crease made in step 10, then unfold.

12 Fold bottom right corner to crease made in step 11.

13 Fold bottom right corner to center diagonal crease.

14 Gently unfold where indicated by arrow.

Finished!

15 Finished petal. Repeat with remaining 4 papers.

Put it together

1 Insert triangular flap from one petal into the triangular slot on the next. Lightly glue into place.

2 Connect all 5 petals.

3 Fan out into blossom shape.

4 Insert flap from last petal into slot of the first and glue into place.

Finished!

61

23 Serving Paper (photo pg 43)

Paper size : 23 x 23 cm

Finished size : 15 x 30 cm

> **Note :** Simply fold paper in half. Thick craft or *washi* paper is best.

25 Toothpick Holder (photo pg 43)

Paper size : 11 x 11 cm

Finished size : 11.5 x 2.5 cm

> **Note :** It's not easy to fold the bottom point over and over, but do your best to crease thoroughly.

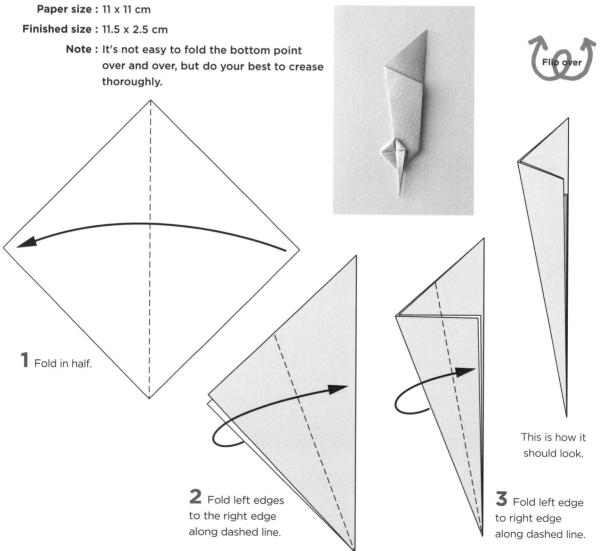

1 Fold in half.

2 Fold left edges to the right edge along dashed line.

3 Fold left edge to right edge along dashed line.

This is how it should look.

Flip over

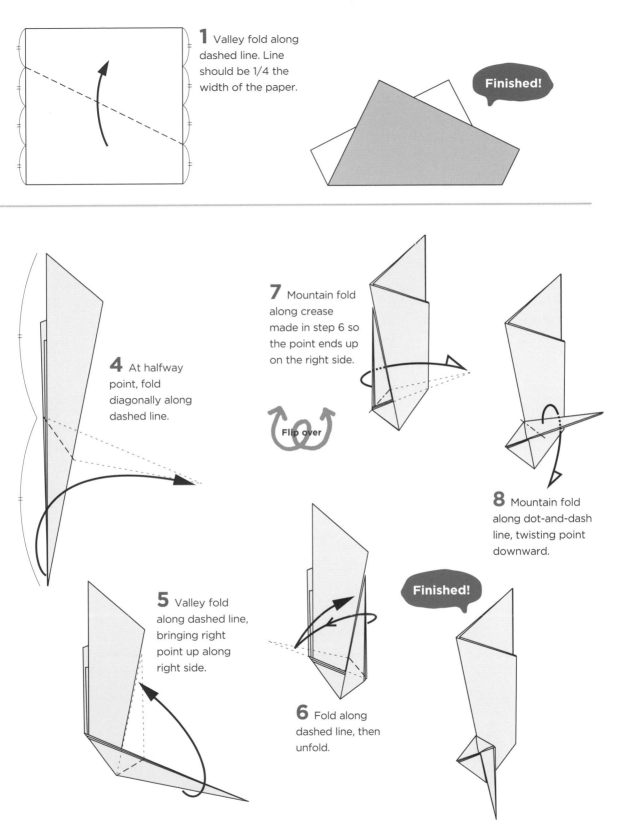

1 Valley fold along dashed line. Line should be 1/4 the width of the paper.

Finished!

4 At halfway point, fold diagonally along dashed line.

7 Mountain fold along crease made in step 6 so the point ends up on the right side.

Flip over

8 Mountain fold along dot-and-dash line, twisting point downward.

5 Valley fold along dashed line, bringing right point up along right side.

6 Fold along dashed line, then unfold.

Finished!

26 Herb Pouch (photo pg 44)

Paper size : Large 12 x 12 cm Small 10 x 10 cm

Finished size : Large 4.3 x 6 cm Small 3.3 x 4.7 cm

Note : This is based on a very old traditional design. Try using transparent or sheer paper so you can easily see the contents.

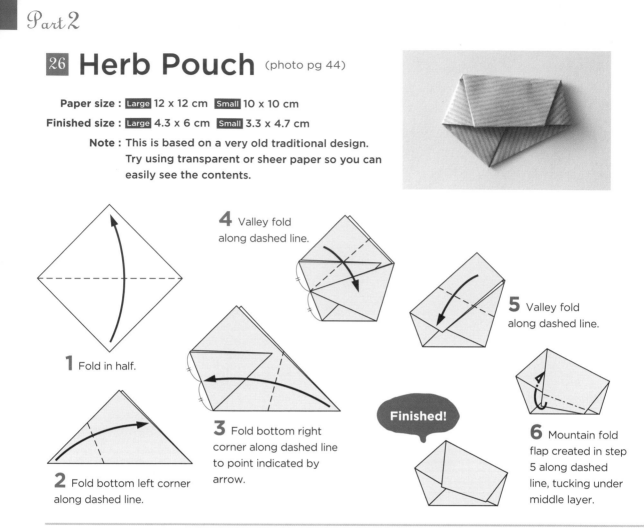

1 Fold in half.

2 Fold bottom left corner along dashed line.

3 Fold bottom right corner along dashed line to point indicated by arrow.

4 Valley fold along dashed line.

5 Valley fold along dashed line.

Finished!

6 Mountain fold flap created in step 5 along dashed line, tucking under middle layer.

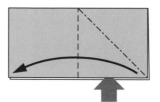

28 Pepper Pouch (photo pg 45)

Paper size : 10 x 10 cm

Finished size : 5 x 5 cm

Note : This version has a diamond in the middle. This gets bulky, so use lighter craft paper.

1 Fold in half.

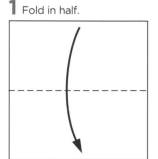

2 Squash fold where indicated by the arrow.

3 Repeat squash fold on reverse side.

Turn 180°

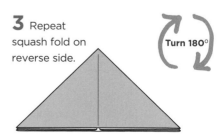

27 Triangle Pouch (photo pg 45)

Paper size : Large 6 x 20.5 cm Small 4 x 14 cm

Finished size : Large 6 x 7 cm Small 4 x 4.8 cm

Note : A simple pouch made by folding along diagonal lines. I made this using brightly colored tracing paper.

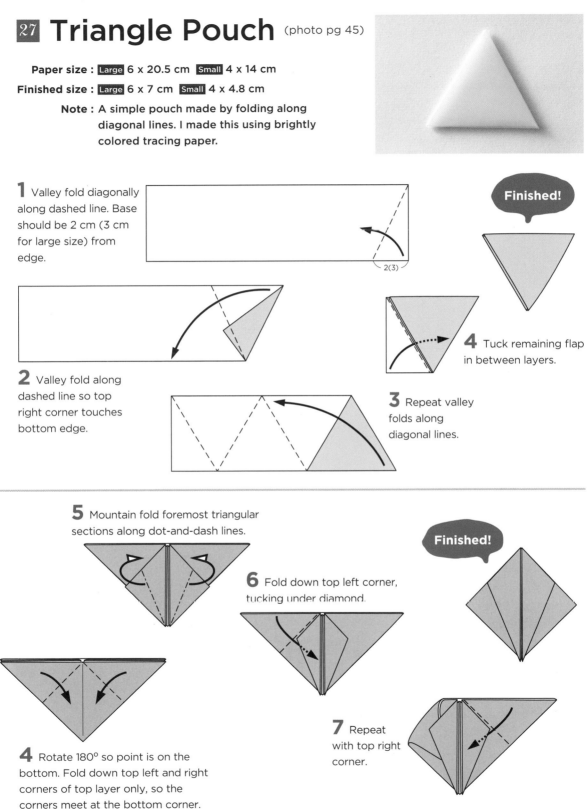

1 Valley fold diagonally along dashed line. Base should be 2 cm (3 cm for large size) from edge.

2(3)

2 Valley fold along dashed line so top right corner touches bottom edge.

3 Repeat valley folds along diagonal lines.

4 Tuck remaining flap in between layers.

Finished!

5 Mountain fold foremost triangular sections along dot-and-dash lines.

6 Fold down top left corner, tucking under diamond.

Finished!

4 Rotate 180° so point is on the bottom. Fold down top left and right corners of top layer only, so the corners meet at the bottom corner.

7 Repeat with top right corner.

65

29 Candy Dish (photo pg 46)

Paper size : Large 25 x 25 cm Small 20.5 x 20.5 cm
Finished size : Large 10.5 x 10.5 x 4 cm
  Small 8.5 x 8.5 x 3.5 cm
Note : The final folds show off the reverse side of the paper.

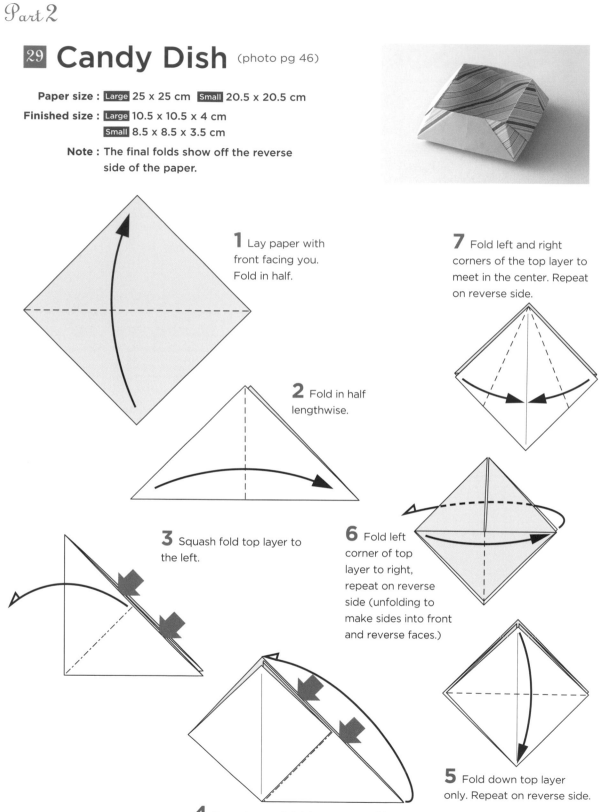

1 Lay paper with front facing you. Fold in half.

2 Fold in half lengthwise.

3 Squash fold top layer to the left.

4 Repeat squash fold on reverse side.

5 Fold down top layer only. Repeat on reverse side.

6 Fold left corner of top layer to right, repeat on reverse side (unfolding to make sides into front and reverse faces.)

7 Fold left and right corners of the top layer to meet in the center. Repeat on reverse side.

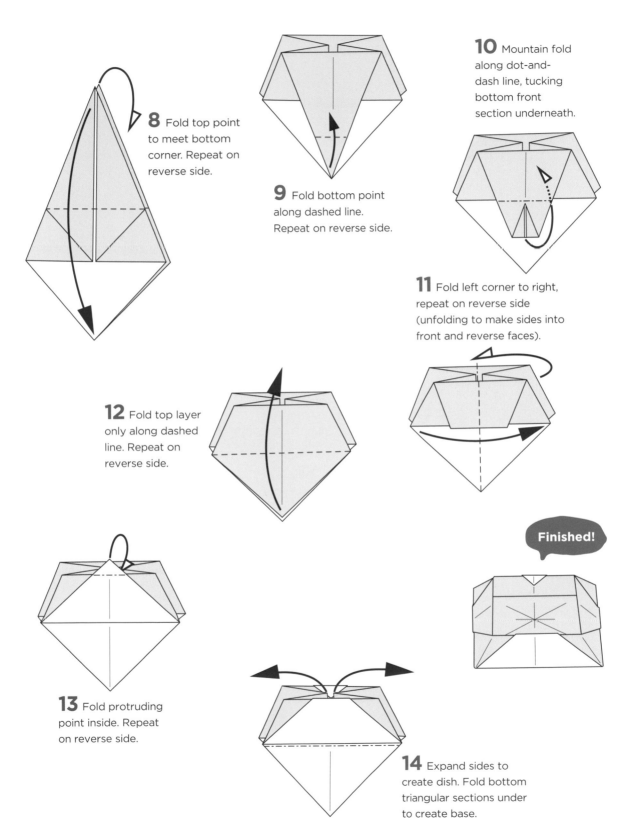

8 Fold top point to meet bottom corner. Repeat on reverse side.

9 Fold bottom point along dashed line. Repeat on reverse side.

10 Mountain fold along dot-and-dash line, tucking bottom front section underneath.

11 Fold left corner to right, repeat on reverse side (unfolding to make sides into front and reverse faces).

12 Fold top layer only along dashed line. Repeat on reverse side.

Finished!

13 Fold protruding point inside. Repeat on reverse side.

14 Expand sides to create dish. Fold bottom triangular sections under to create base.

67

30 Candy Box (photo pg 47)

Paper size : Large 20 x 20 cm Small 17 x 17 cm

Finished size : Large 10 x 10 x 5.3 cm
Small 8.5 x 8.5 x 4.7 cm

Note : The reverse side of the paper will show as the border around the opening of the box, so try making this with paper with a pattern on the front and a solid reverse.

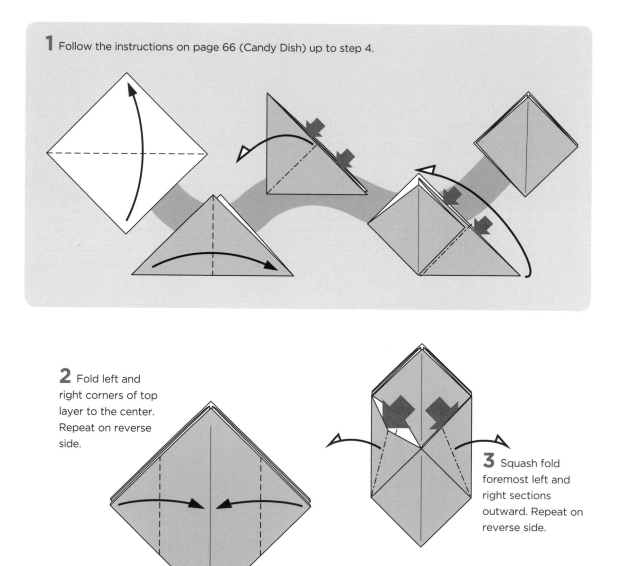

1 Follow the instructions on page 66 (Candy Dish) up to step 4.

2 Fold left and right corners of top layer to the center. Repeat on reverse side.

3 Squash fold foremost left and right sections outward. Repeat on reverse side.

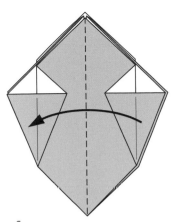

4 Fold left corner to right, repeat on reverse side (unfolding to make sides into front and reverse faces).

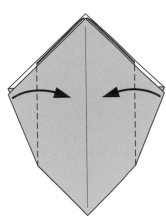

5 Valley fold left and right sides along dashed lines. Repeat on reverse side.

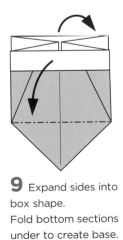

6 Fold top layer down along dashed line. Repeat on reverse side.

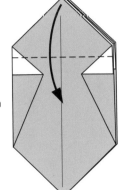

7 Fold front edge along dashed line. Repeat on reverse side.

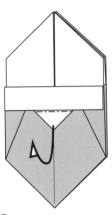

8 Tuck top triangle under flap. Repeat on reverse side. Repeat steps 6 through 8 with left and right sides.

9 Expand sides into box shape. Fold bottom sections under to create base.

Finished!

31 Cutlery Rest (photo pg 48)

Paper size : 10 x 10 cm

Finished size : 2.5 x 6 x 2.3 cm

Note : This creates a long pyramid shape. Make sure to follow the diagram closely to create a stable base.

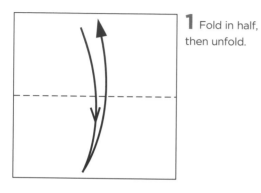

1 Fold in half, then unfold.

2 Fold top and bottom edges to the center, then unfold.

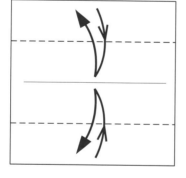

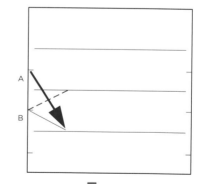

6 Repeat step 4 on the right side, with points E and F.

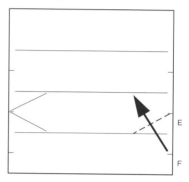

5 Hold down paper at point B, fold point A to bottom crease, creasing along dashed line, then unfold.

3 Mark half-way points between creases as indicated by letters on the diagram.

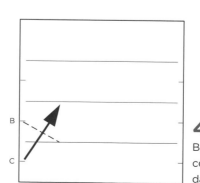

4 Hold down paper at point B, fold up point C to the center crease, creasing along dashed line, then unfold.

8 Valley fold left and right edges along dashed lines.

9 Mountain fold top layer along dot-and-dash lines, folding up into a pyramid shape with point B as the top (on the left) and point E as the top (on the right).

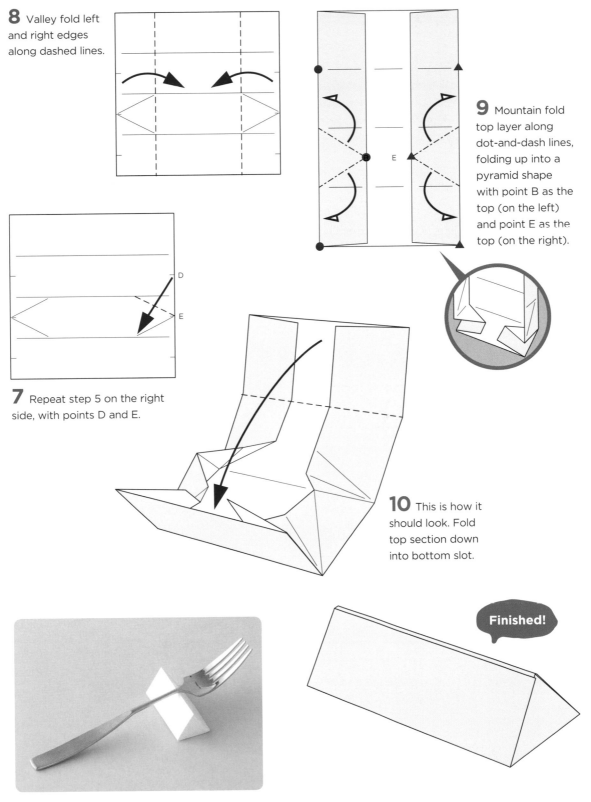

7 Repeat step 5 on the right side, with points D and E.

10 This is how it should look. Fold top section down into bottom slot.

Finished!

32 Heart Napkin Ring (photo pg 48)

Paper size : 19 x 19 cm

Finished size : Heart 6 x 4.8 cm

Ring 5.5 cm (diameter)

Note : One sheet of paper turns into a ring
decorated with a heart.

1 Fold in half widthwise, then unfold; fold in half lengthwise, then unfold.

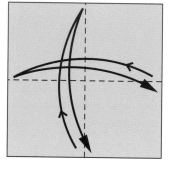

2 Fold down top edge along top dashed line, then again along second dashed line, rolling the paper down.

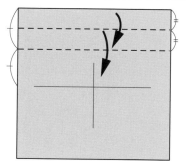

3 Mountain fold left and right sides along dot-and-dash lines, so corners meet in the center on the back.

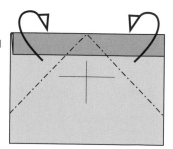

Flip over

4 Fold top triangular section backwards along dot-and-dash line.

5 Mountain fold top folded section then squash fold upwards.

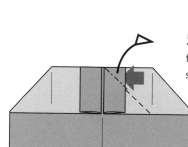

6 Repeat on left side.

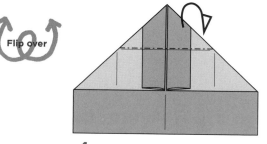

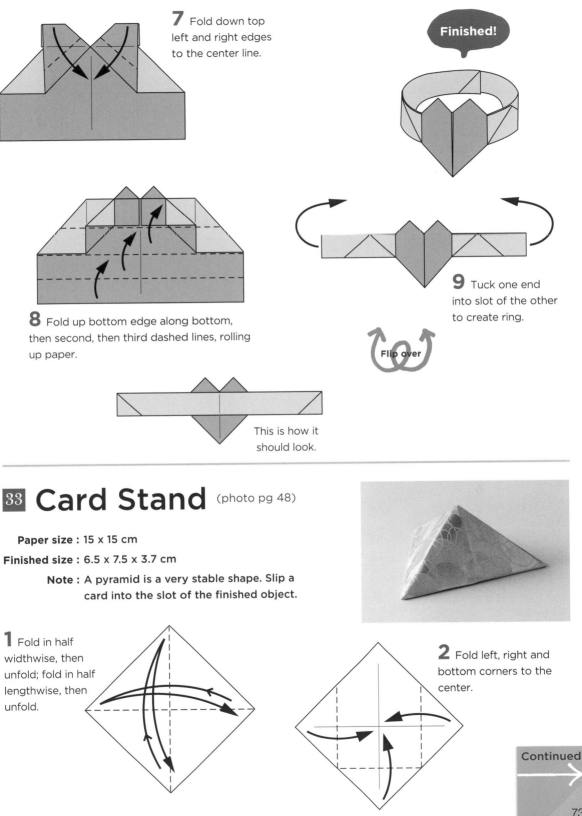

7 Fold down top left and right edges to the center line.

Finished!

8 Fold up bottom edge along bottom, then second, then third dashed lines, rolling up paper.

9 Tuck one end into slot of the other to create ring.

Flip over

This is how it should look.

33 Card Stand (photo pg 48)

Paper size : 15 x 15 cm

Finished size : 6.5 x 7.5 x 3.7 cm

Note : A pyramid is a very stable shape. Slip a card into the slot of the finished object.

1 Fold in half widthwise, then unfold; fold in half lengthwise, then unfold.

2 Fold left, right and bottom corners to the center.

Continued →

Continued from
previous page

3 Fold bottom left
and right corners to the
center.

4 Fold in half.

5 Valley fold
along dashed line.

6 Expand sides
of the bottom
triangular section.

7 Fold down
top right point
along dashed
line and tuck
inward to the
center.

8 Fold down top
triangular section
along dashed line
and tuck inward to
the center, creating a
bottomless pyramid.

Finished!

This is where the
card goes.

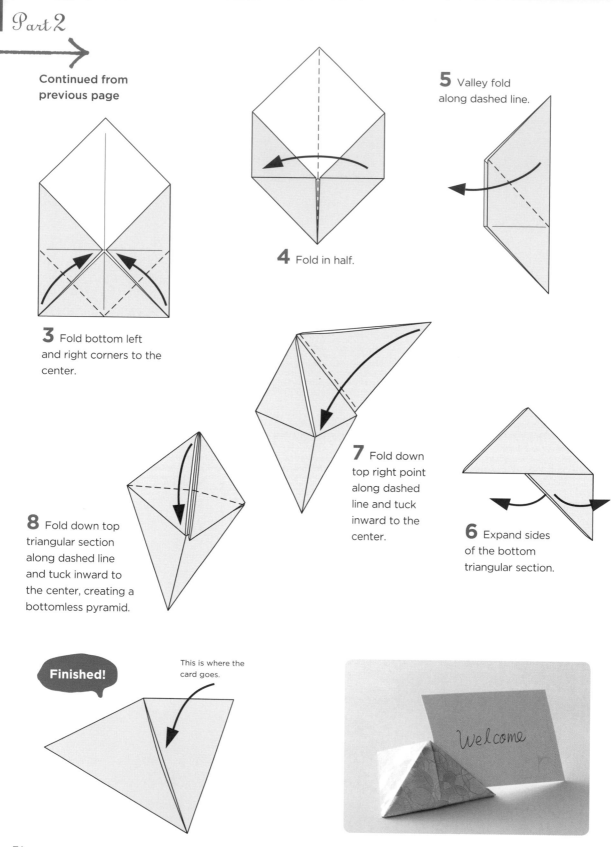

34 Photo Frame (photo pg 49)

Paper size : Square 28 x 28 cm Rectangle 26 x 30 cm

Finished size : Square 14 x 14 cm Rectangle 13 x 15 cm

Note : The final frame will be half the size of the paper, so make sure to use paper large enough to fit the photo. The folding pattern is the same for both the square and rectangular frames.

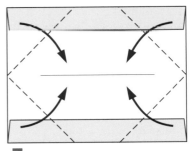

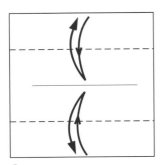

1 Fold in half widthwise, then unfold. Fold top and bottom edges to the center crease, then unfold.

2 Fold top and bottom edges along dashed lines.

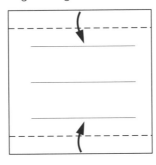

3 Fold all four corners to the center crease.

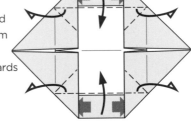

4 Squash fold top and bottom edges where indicated towards the center.

5 Fold left and right triangular sections to the center.

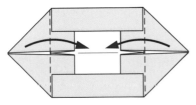

Finished!

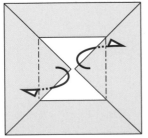

6 Mountain fold along dot-and-dash lines, tucking triangular sections under.

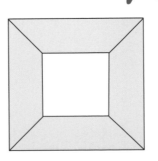

Part 3

Gift Wrappings with a Japanese Twist

35 **Cross Pouch**

Instructions ······ **84**

A gift bag to show your feelings of
connection with the giftee.

Use this pouch when gifting money, or use
to store seeds or herbs.
This traditional wrapping can be used for
all kinds of things.

This is a playful riff on the traditional "thread holder" design. These make cute, pudgy pouches.

Instructions ······ **86**

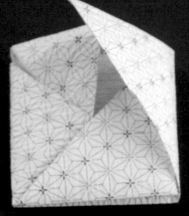

36 **Cross-Over Pouch**

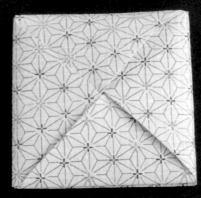

Adorable, traditional gift wrappings.

These are super easy to whip up in no time, making them great for last-minute gifts or a delicate way to leave notes or tips. The ribbon on the bottom pouch is made from textured paper and decorated with stamps. Try dressing these up with fun prints or stickers.

Instructions **94**

37 **Simple Pouch**

A whimsical version of gift-wrapping.

Add wings to finely designed paper.

Pinwheel Pouches

This design where the folds are stacked is based on a traditional kimono-wrapping design. 39 and 40 are variations on 38.

Instructions ······ **94**

41 Four-Corner Pouch
Instructions ······ **88**

Use modern patterns for a whole new take
on traditional origami designs.

Lovely kimono-wrapping folds are used to make
these four- and six-sided pouches.
It's a traditional Japanese technique, but feel free
to use all kinds of paper with any type of pattern.

42 Hexagonal Pouch
Instructions ······ **90**

Add these beauties to your coaster collection.

43 Octagonal Pouch

These pouches fold up nice and flat,
making them very suitable for coasters
or saucers. Make these in charming
patterns to set the stage for tea time.

Instructions ······**92**

Celebratory Envelopes

44 Instructions ······ **97**

45 Instructions ······ **98**

Think congratulatory thoughts while folding these envelopes.

Sure, you can pick up envelopes at any drugstore, but that's what
makes handmade ones all the more special. Choose paper that suits
the person you're making it for and fold it up with feelings of congrats.

Use colors that pop so they know just who these are from.

46 Instructions ⋯⋯ **100**

47 Instructions ⋯⋯ **101**

Use bright, bold colors if the giftees are good friends.
Add small details and flourishes to make them feel as
unique as they are.

35 Cross Pouch (photo pg 76)

Paper size : 20 x 15 cm

Finished size : 8.5 x 7 cm

Note : Use paper with contrasting colors on each side to make the cross pattern stand out.

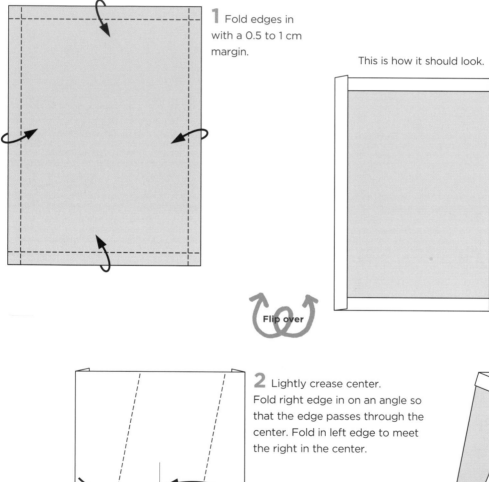

1 Fold edges in with a 0.5 to 1 cm margin.

This is how it should look.

Flip over

2 Lightly crease center. Fold right edge in on an angle so that the edge passes through the center. Fold in left edge to meet the right in the center.

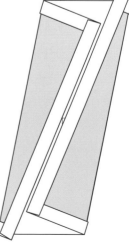

3 This is how it should look. Unfold back to the beginning of step 2.

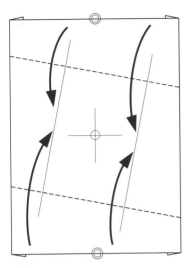

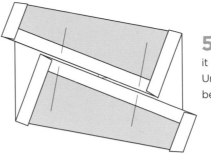

5 This is how it should look. Unfold back to the beginning of step 4.

4 Fold top and bottom edges at a 90° angle to the creases made in step 2, making sure edges meet in the center.

6 Fold edges in order listed in the diagram.

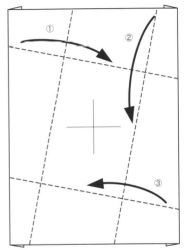

This is how it should look.

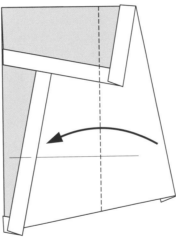

7 Fold along dashed line, then unfold.

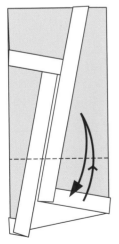

Finished!

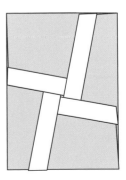

8 Fold left half of bottom section under left-hand flap.

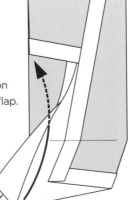

36 Cross-Over Pouch (photo pg 77)

Paper size : 21 x 21 cm

Finished size : 7 x 7 cm

> **Note :** When using this for wrapping, finish folding then unfold back to step 2. Place object in the middle, then fold again.

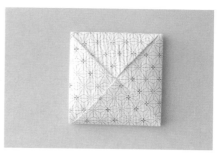

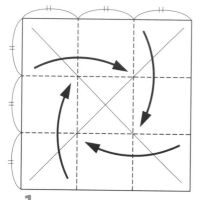

1 Fold in half along diagonal lines as shown in diagram, then unfold. Fold in thirds along dashed lines, then unfold.

Flip over

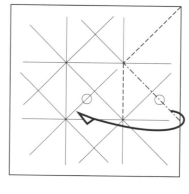

3 Mountain fold along dot-and-dash lines, matching points marked with red circles and valley folding along dashed line.

Flip over

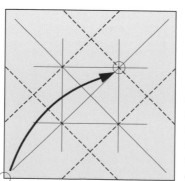

2 Fold corner to point marked with red circle, then unfold. Repeat with remaining 3 corners.

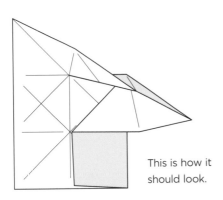

This is how it should look.

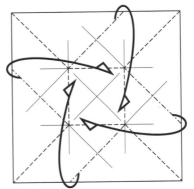

4 Continue mountain folds in succession, folding corners toward the center.

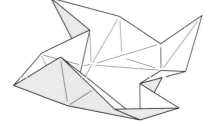

This is how it should look.

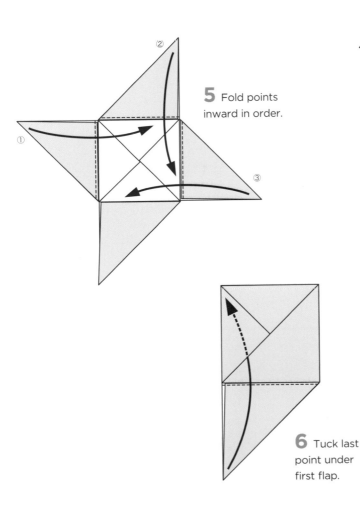

5 Fold points inward in order.

6 Tuck last point under first flap.

Finished!

44 Four-Corner Pouch (photo pg 80)

Paper size : 16 x 16 cm

Finished size : 7 x 7 cm

Note : Creasing carefully makes this easy to fold. Keep the paper oriented the same way as the diagrams and make a note of the next step before folding and you'll be just fine.

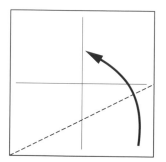

1 Crease along lines as shown in the diagram. Fold along dashed line running from the opposite corner to the horizontal crease.

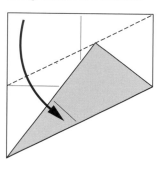

2 Fold top left corner along dashed line likewise.

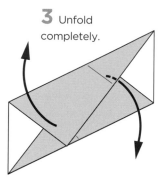

3 Unfold completely.

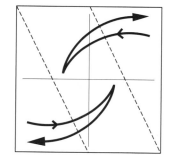

4 Fold left and right sides in the same manner as in steps 1 and 2, folding along dashed lines, then unfolding.

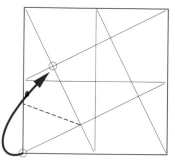

5 Fold up lower left corner (marked with a red circle) so it touches the other red circle.

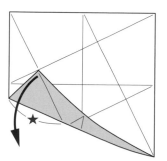

6 Only crease along section marked with a red star, then unfold.

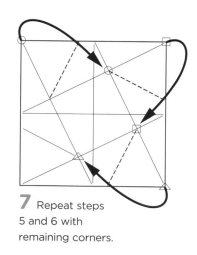

7 Repeat steps 5 and 6 with remaining corners.

8 This is how it should look. Fold bottom right corner along dashed line.

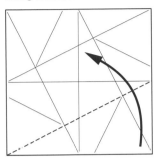

9 Using the creases, line up points with matching symbols, mountain and valley folding where indicated.

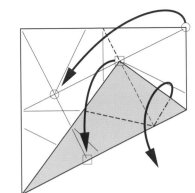

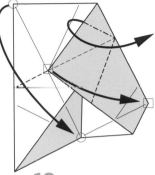

10 Line up points with matching symbols, mountain and valley folding where indicated.

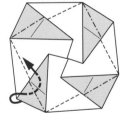

11 Continue this process.

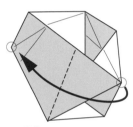

12 Fold along dashed line, lining up points marked with red circles.

13 Pull out left bottom corner. Fold left side under bottom flap.

Lift up left side and pull out corner hidden underneath.

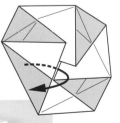

Replace left side, tucking under unfolded bottom corner.

14 Inside reverse fold all 4 corners.

Finished!

42 Hexagonal Pouch (photo pg 80)

Paper size : 17 x 17 cm

Finished size : 8 to 9 cm

Note : Make the cut in step 6 as clean as possible to create a nice hexagonal shape.

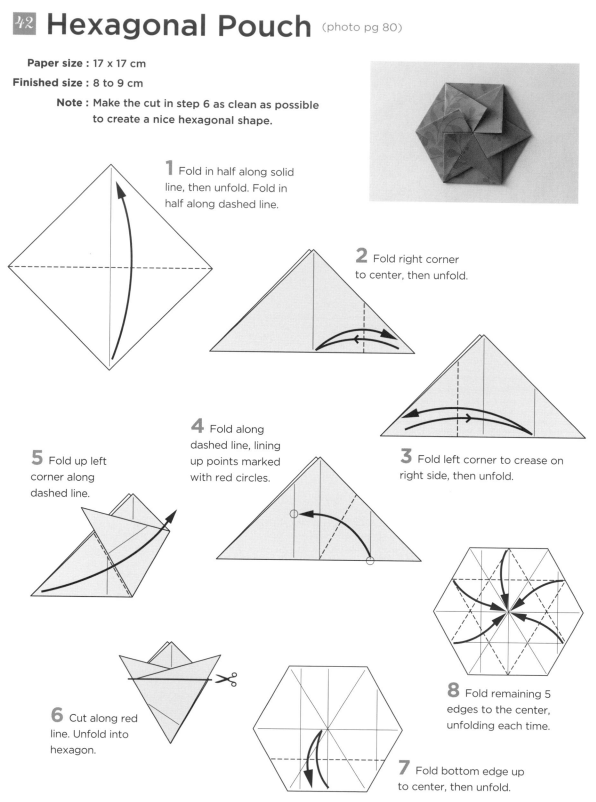

1 Fold in half along solid line, then unfold. Fold in half along dashed line.

2 Fold right corner to center, then unfold.

3 Fold left corner to crease on right side, then unfold.

4 Fold along dashed line, lining up points marked with red circles.

5 Fold up left corner along dashed line.

6 Cut along red line. Unfold into hexagon.

7 Fold bottom edge up to center, then unfold.

8 Fold remaining 5 edges to the center, unfolding each time.

11 Repeat squash fold with lower right side. Continue squash folding with remaining sides.

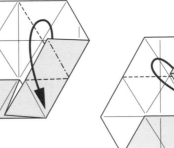

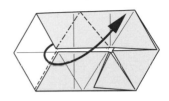

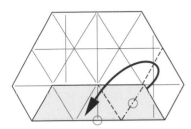

10 Mountain and valley fold where indicated, lining up points marked with red circles to create a squash fold.

9 Fold up bottom edge to the center.

12 With final squash fold, pull out inside corner so it overlaps bottom flap.

13 Fold bottom triangular section to left corner.

Finished!

14 Squash fold top left section downward.

15 This is how it should look. Repeat squash folds with remaining sides.

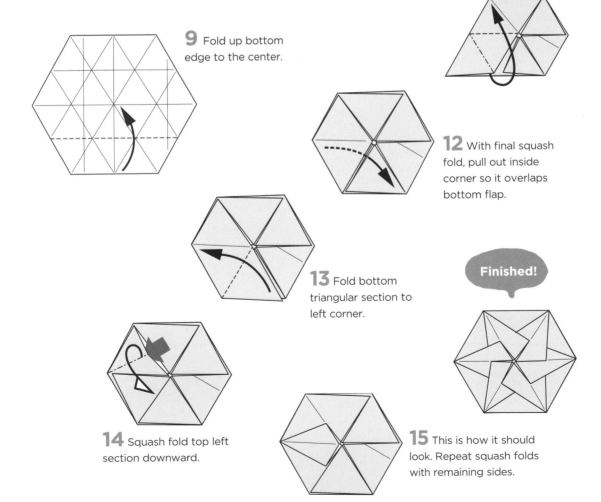

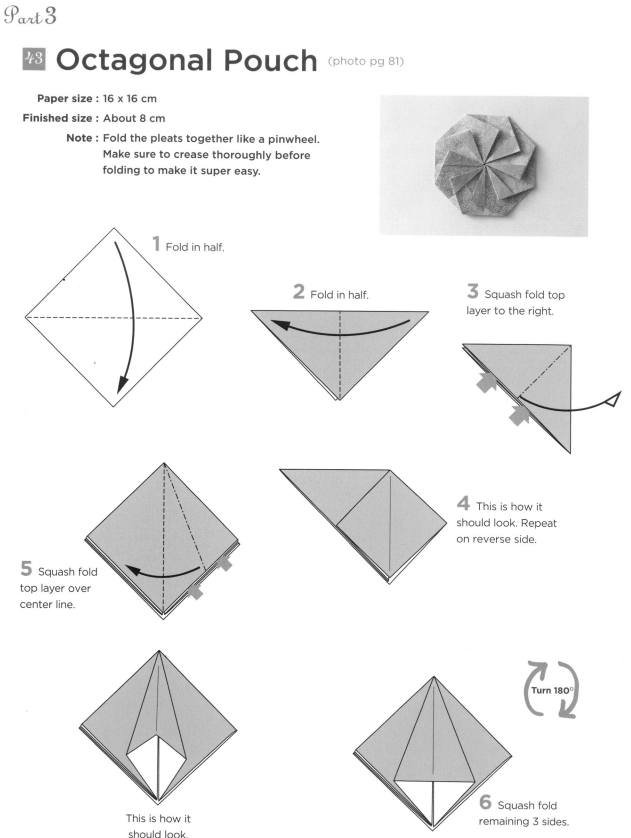

43 Octagonal Pouch (photo pg 81)

Paper size : 16 x 16 cm

Finished size : About 8 cm

Note : Fold the pleats together like a pinwheel. Make sure to crease thoroughly before folding to make it super easy.

1 Fold in half.

2 Fold in half.

3 Squash fold top layer to the right.

4 This is how it should look. Repeat on reverse side.

5 Squash fold top layer over center line.

This is how it should look.

Turn 180°

6 Squash fold remaining 3 sides.

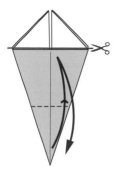

7 Cut along red line. Fold in half along dashed line, then unfold.

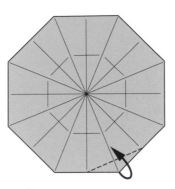

8 Unfold into octagon. Fold bottom right corner along dashed line.

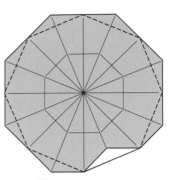

9 Repeat with remaining corners.

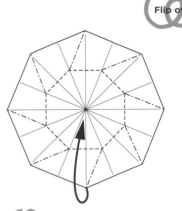

Flip over

11 This is how one corner folded should look. Fold next pleat over the first.

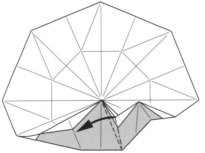

10 Re-crease along dashed lines. Mountain fold along dot-and-dash lines, folding edges toward the center.

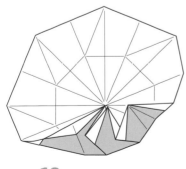

12 Continue folding pleats.

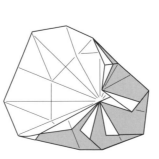

Finished!

37 Simple Pouch (photo pg 78)

Paper size : 16 x 20 cm

Finished size : 7 x 7 cm

Note : Fix with stickers or tie with a ribbon to make giving this gift as fun as it is to receive.

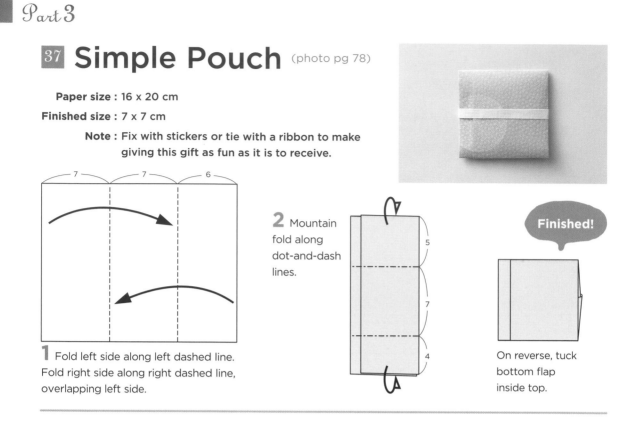

1 Fold left side along left dashed line. Fold right side along right dashed line, overlapping left side.

2 Mountain fold along dot-and-dash lines.

Finished!

On reverse, tuck bottom flap inside top.

---

38 39 40 Pinwheel Pouches (photo pg 79)

Paper size : 15 x 15 cm

Finished size : 8 x 8 cm

Note : The finished shape will show the reverse side, so keep that in mind when choosing paper. All 3 designs are basically the same, with variations in step 2.

Basic design 38

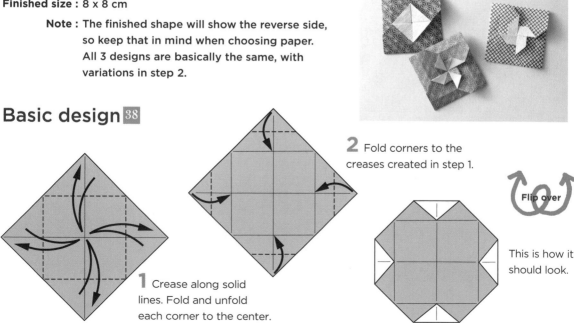

1 Crease along solid lines. Fold and unfold each corner to the center.

2 Fold corners to the creases created in step 1.

Flip over

This is how it should look.

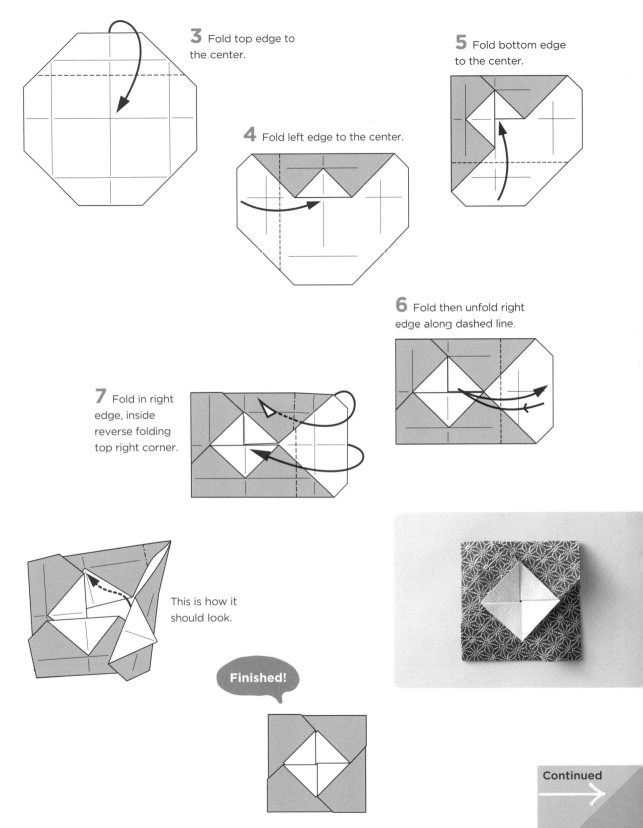

3 Fold top edge to the center.

4 Fold left edge to the center.

5 Fold bottom edge to the center.

6 Fold then unfold right edge along dashed line.

7 Fold in right edge, inside reverse folding top right corner.

This is how it should look.

Finished!

Continued →

Part 3

→ Variation on step 2 of basic design

39 Step 2

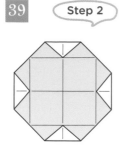

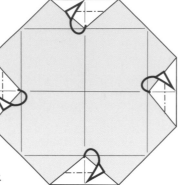

Mountain fold along dot-and-dash lines, tucking points under. Finish steps for basic shape.

Finished!

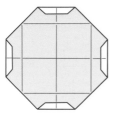

Flip over

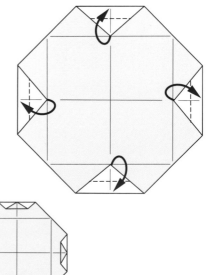

40

Step 2

Valley fold along dashed lines. Finish steps for basic shape.

Finished!

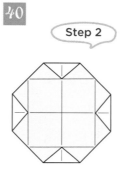

Flip over

44 Celebratory Envelope (photo pg 82)

Paper size : 30 x 30 cm

Finished size : 18 x 10 cm

Note : This design shows off the pattern of the paper, so try papers with bold prints. Choose the side you want to showcase before folding.

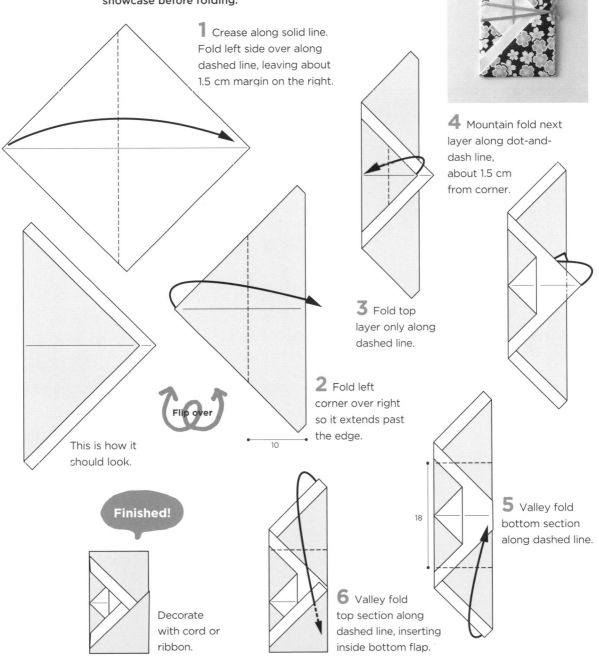

1 Crease along solid line. Fold left side over along dashed line, leaving about 1.5 cm margin on the right.

4 Mountain fold next layer along dot-and-dash line, about 1.5 cm from corner.

3 Fold top layer only along dashed line.

2 Fold left corner over right so it extends past the edge.

10

Flip over

This is how it should look.

5 Valley fold bottom section along dashed line.

18

Finished!

Decorate with cord or ribbon.

6 Valley fold top section along dashed line, inserting inside bottom flap.

45 Celebratory Envelope (photo pg 82)

Paper size : `Main` 43 x 36 cm
`Inserts` A: 10 x 5 cm, B: 9 x 5 cm, C: 3 x 3 cm

Finished size : 18 x 10 cm

Note : Formal Japanese celebratory envelopes use thick danshi paper (medium weight and finely textured with wrinkles). If you find danshi paper, it'll make the final product look very elegant.

1 Measure and crease where indicated on the diagram.

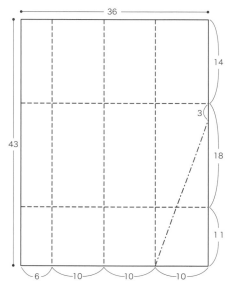

2 Fold along dashed line.

6 Fold back the top section, followed by the bottom section along the dot-and-dash lines.

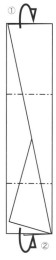

3 Fold corner back along crease created by mountain fold in step 1.

4 Fold in order according to diagram.

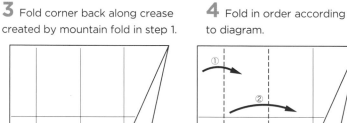

5 Fold right side over.

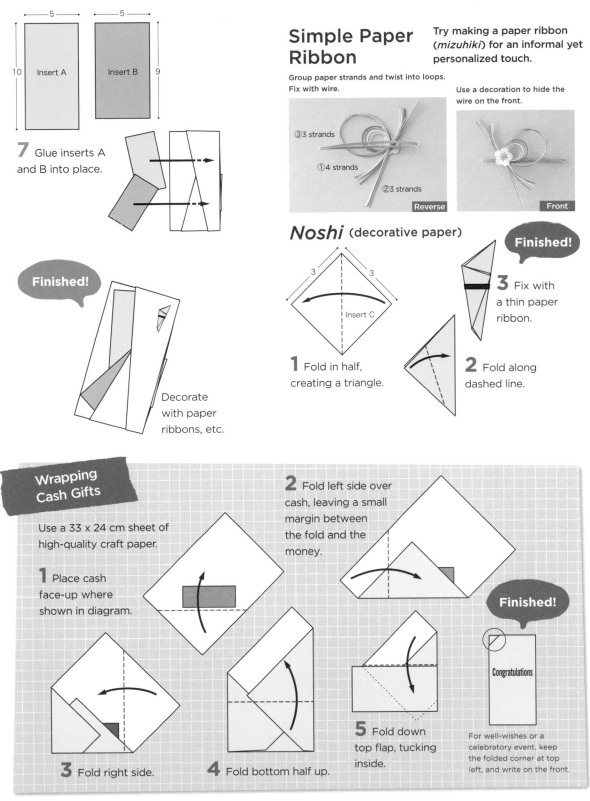

5 — 5

Insert A | Insert B

10 | 9

7 Glue inserts A and B into place.

Finished!

Decorate with paper ribbons, etc.

Simple Paper Ribbon

Try making a paper ribbon (*mizuhiki*) for an informal yet personalized touch.

Group paper strands and twist into loops. Fix with wire.

③3 strands

①4 strands

②3 strands

Reverse

Use a decoration to hide the wire on the front.

Front

Noshi (decorative paper)

3 — 3

Insert C

1 Fold in half, creating a triangle.

2 Fold along dashed line.

3 Fix with a thin paper ribbon.

Finished!

Wrapping Cash Gifts

Use a 33 x 24 cm sheet of high-quality craft paper.

1 Place cash face-up where shown in diagram.

2 Fold left side over cash, leaving a small margin between the fold and the money.

3 Fold right side.

4 Fold bottom half up.

5 Fold down top flap, tucking inside.

Finished!

Congratulations

For well-wishes or a celebratory event, keep the folded corner at top left, and write on the front.

46 Celebratory Envelope (photo pg 83)

Paper size : Main 40 x 30 cm Insert 40 x 10.5 cm

Finished size : 18 x 10 cm

Note : This is a very simple design, so dress it up with fun patterned papers and color combinations.
Be sure to use fairly heavy paper for the main part.

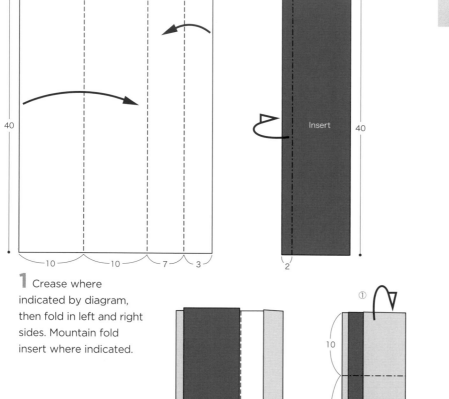

1 Crease where indicated by diagram, then fold in left and right sides. Mountain fold insert where indicated.

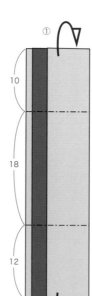

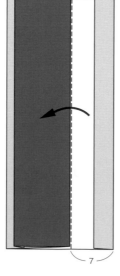

2 Place insert (with fold on the left) on top of the main paper and fold main paper along dashed line.

3 Fold down top section; fold up bottom section.

Finished!

Decorate with a ribbon, etc.

47 Celebratory Envelope (photo pg 83)

Paper size : Main 40 x 30 cm
Inserts A: 40 x 6 cm, B: 40 x 5 cm, Lace: 40 cm

Finished size : 18 x 10 cm

Note : Since this version uses lace, try using heavy paper with embossing or other subtle decorations for the main paper.

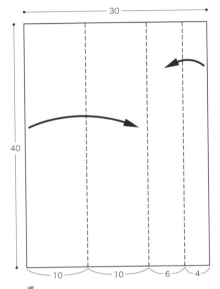

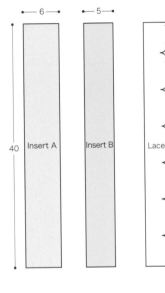

1 Crease where indicated by diagram, then fold in left and right sides.

2 Layer inserts A and B on the left side. Glue lace on the right edge, then fold along dashed line.

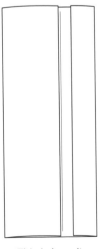

This is how it should look.

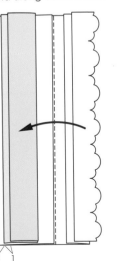

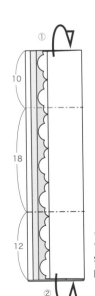

3 Fold down top section; fold up bottom section.

Finished!

Decorate with lace or artificial flowers.

Part 4
Desktop Accessories

48 Book Cover 1
Instructions ···· **112**

Protect your paperbacks! Add a layer to
stow your bookmarks. Use strips of lace
as bookmarks, too.

Create a special cover for the books that are important to you.

49 Book Cover 2

Instructions ····· **113**

50 Book Cover 3

Instructions ····· **114**

Stuff these envelopes full of feelings.

51 **Envelope**

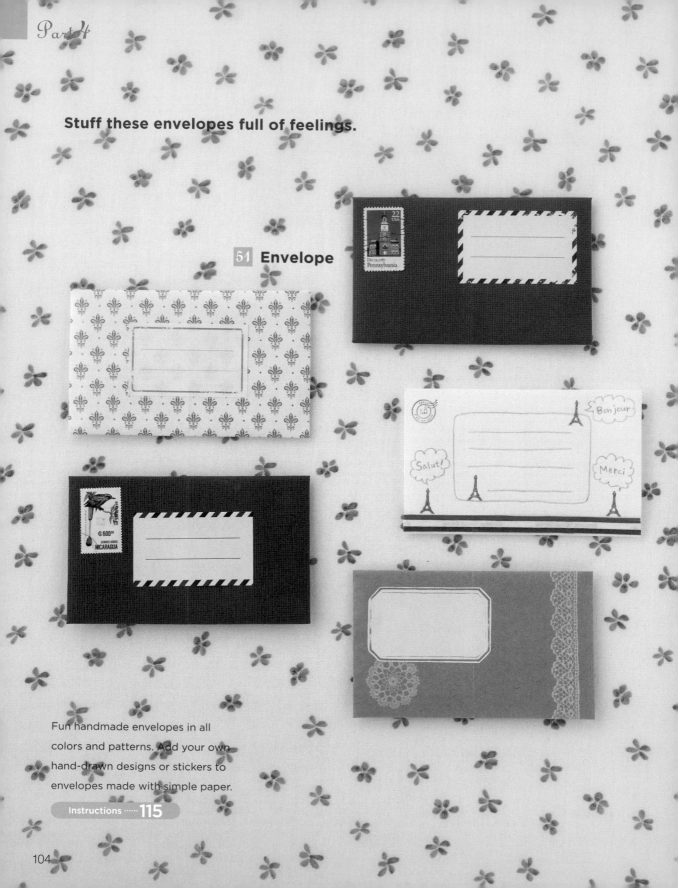

Fun handmade envelopes in all colors and patterns. Add your own hand-drawn designs or stickers to envelopes made with simple paper.

Instructions ······ **115**

Make these wrappings stand out form the crowd with a whimsical necktie accent.

53 Shirt and Tie Bag
Instructions ······ **118**

54 Shirt and Tie Envelope
Instructions ······ **116**

These fun gift wrappings are easy to tailor to the giftee. Use the envelope version for photos or other flat items.

Create keepsake cases for your favorite CDs.

54 CD Case

If you create a photo album or music mix as
a gift, sending it in just a plastic case is dull.
Add buttons for a real home-made feel.

Instructions ······120

Professionals know how to keep their desks organized.

These items will help keep the chaos
on your desk organized. Try making
them in all sizes to suit your needs.

**The scent of potpourri wafts
from the tiny windows.**

57 **Pyramid Potpourri Case**

This pyramid-shaped case is adorable.
Fill these up with your favorite
potpourri mix and enjoy.

Instructions ⸱⸱⸱⸱⸱⸱**122**

Show off your flair for decorating with a sweet tissue case.

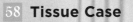 **58 Tissue Case**

Don't leave home without a pack of tissues. With a case as fashionable as this you'll always want to keep them handy.

Instructions ······ **123**

Craft all kinds with varied colors and patterns to suit your mood.

59 **Card Case**

Keep your cards handy with this simple case. Try making several and switch them up when you want a change of pace.

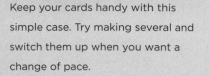

Instructions ······**124**

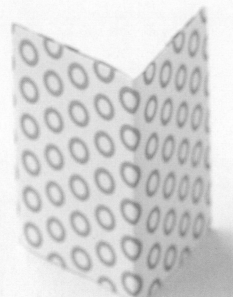

60 Folding Card Case

Change your card case depending on the situation.

Use different card cases for different events. The bifold design keeps the cards safely inside.

Instructions ⋯⋯ **126**

48 Book Cover 1 (photo pg 102)

Paper size : Measure book, doubling width. Add 14 cm to the height and 10 cm to the width.

Finished size : Custom

Note : This design creates a pocket in which you can store bookmarks. Since the pocket will show the reverse side, use paper that has designs on both sides.

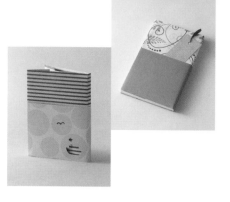

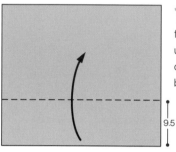

1 Place paper with front facing you. Fold up bottom edge along dashed line. (This will become the pocket.)

9.5

Flip over

2 Fold down top edge along dashed line.

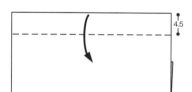

4.5

3 Fold in right edge.

5

This is how it should look.

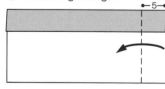

Finished!

6 Slide book's front cover in between left flaps.

5 Wrap book. Fold left side along front cover edge of the book.

Optional

Place a bookmark in the pocket. If you cut a shape out of the pocket section you can see the base.

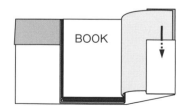

BOOK

4 Slide book's back cover in between right flaps.

49 Book Cover 2 (photo pg 103)

Paper size : Measure book, doubling width. Add 9 cm to the height and 20 cm to the width.

Finished size : Custom

Note : This is a basic book cover. Use your favorite paper to wrap your favorite books!

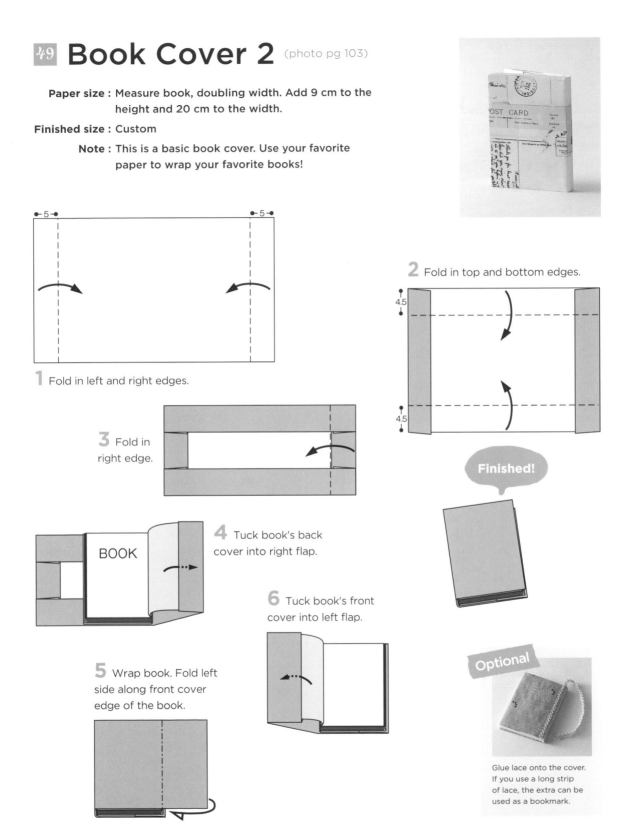

1 Fold in left and right edges.

2 Fold in top and bottom edges.

3 Fold in right edge.

Finished!

4 Tuck book's back cover into right flap.

BOOK

6 Tuck book's front cover into left flap.

5 Wrap book. Fold left side along front cover edge of the book.

Optional

Glue lace onto the cover. If you use a long strip of lace, the extra can be used as a bookmark.

50 Book Cover 3 (photo pg 103)

Paper size : Measure book, doubling width. Add 9 cm to the height and 32 cm to the width.

Finished size : Custom

Note : The "step" folding on the sides creates a nice accent. Try using plain, textured paper so the folds stand out.

1 Fold in left and right edges.

Finished!

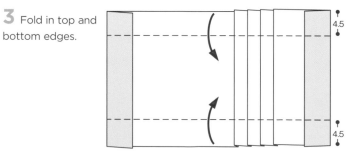

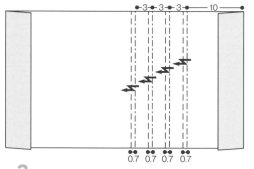

2 Mountain and valley fold right side where indicated (accordion folding).

4 Fold in right edge. Place book inside (as with previous book covers.)

3 Fold in top and bottom edges.

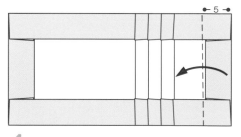

51 Envelope (photo pg 104)

Paper size : 21 x 29.7 cm

Finished size : 9 x 14.8 cm (A4 size)

Note : This makes a standard A4 size envelope. Decorate with stickers or your own drawings to make it unique.

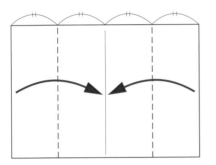

1 Crease along solid line. Fold left and right edges so they meet in the center.

2 Fold top right and left corners so they meet in the center.

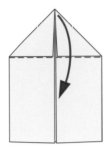

3 Fold top triangle down along dashed line.

4 Fold bottom third along dashed line, then unfold.

5 Fold up bottom left and right corners along dashed lines.

6 Fold up bottom third along dashed line. Tuck top flap into bottom slot.

Finished!

Seal with a sticker or sealing wax.

Optional

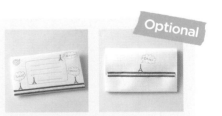

When sending letters from abroad, use paper with local designs.

52 Shirt and Tie Envelope (photo pg 105)

Necktie

Paper size : 12 x 12 cm

Finished size : 12 x 5 cm

Note : The knot has several layers and can be hard to fold, so be sure to crease well.

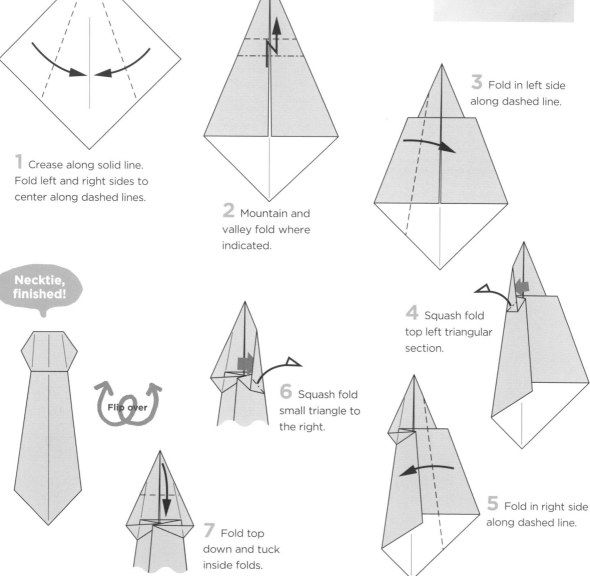

1 Crease along solid line. Fold left and right sides to center along dashed lines.

2 Mountain and valley fold where indicated.

3 Fold in left side along dashed line.

4 Squash fold top left triangular section.

5 Fold in right side along dashed line.

6 Squash fold small triangle to the right.

7 Fold top down and tuck inside folds.

Necktie, finished!

Flip over

Shirt

Paper size : 52 x 26 cm

Finished size : 21.5 x 19.5 cm

Note : This will fit a large photograph. If you want a smaller version, use paper that's 38 x 20 cm, which folds up into 16 x 14.5 cm.

1 Crease along solid line. Fold in left and right edges to center, then unfold.

2 Valley fold bottom left and right corners. Mountain fold top edge (for the collar).

3 Fold in left and right edges.

4 Fold top edge backwards, again. Fold up bottom edge, then unfold.

5 Squash fold bottom inner corners outward.

6 Fold top left and right corners along dashed lines to the center.

7 Fold bottom half up, tucking bottom edge under collar.

Finished!

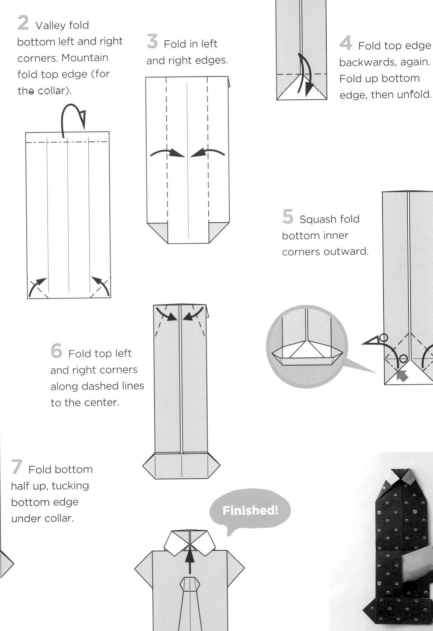

Slide photo inside.

53 Shirt and Tie Bag (photo pg 105)

What you need : Paper bag with a gusset, Necktie (pg 116)

Note : Make a few cuts and folds into an average paper bag to transform it into a dress shirt.

1 Fold down top of bag to create collar.

2 Using the folded edge as a guide, make cuts on the left and right sides.

3 Fold left and right collar parts diagonally toward the center.

Finished!

5 Glue tie into place.

This is how it should look.

4 Mountain fold shoulders.

56 Desktop Box (photo pg 107)

Paper size : Large 28 x 40 cm Small 20.5 x 30 cm
Finished size : Large 10 x 18 x 5 cm Small 7.5 x 13 x 4 cm

Note : This simple-to-make box is very handy. You can use a newspaper insert and turn it into a dust box.

1 Fold in half, then unfold. Fold right and left edges to the center.

2 Fold in half.

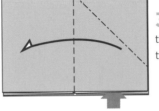

3 Squash fold top right layer to the left.

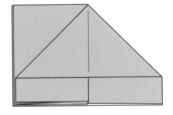

4 This is how it should look. Repeat squash fold on reverse side.

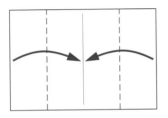

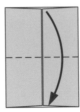

6 Fold left and right sides of top layer only to the center. Repeat on reverse side.

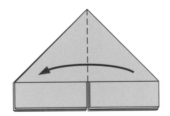

5 Fold top right section over left. Repeat on reverse side.

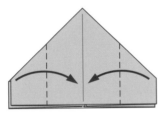

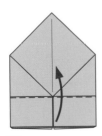

7 Fold bottom section of top layer only upwards.

Turn 180°

8 Expand sides outward. Tuck bottom triangular flaps under to create base.

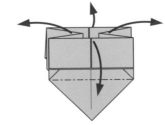

Finished!

119

55 Pen Tray (photo pg 107)

Paper size : 21 x 10 cm

Finished size : 19 x 6 x 1.2 cm

Note : This is basically the same pattern as the Boat Tray (pg 56). The rectangular piece of paper will fold into a long, narrow tray. Switching steps 6 and 7 will give you a different variation.

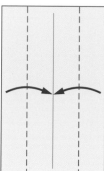

1 Place paper with the side you want to show facing you. Crease along solid line. Fold left and right edges to the center.

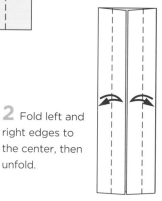

2 Fold left and right edges to the center, then unfold.

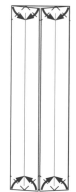

3 Fold in all 8 corners along dashed lines.

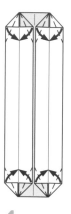

4 Fold new corners along dashed lines.

---

54 CD Case (photo pg 106)

What you need : Ripple board: 35 x 30 cm
2 buttons (2.5 cm diameter)
String: 28 cm; Thread and needle

Finished size: 15 x 15 cm

Note : Try to find corrugated ripple board for the case. Use a craft spatula or stylus to crease before folding.

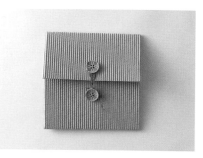

5 Fold center left and right sections outward.

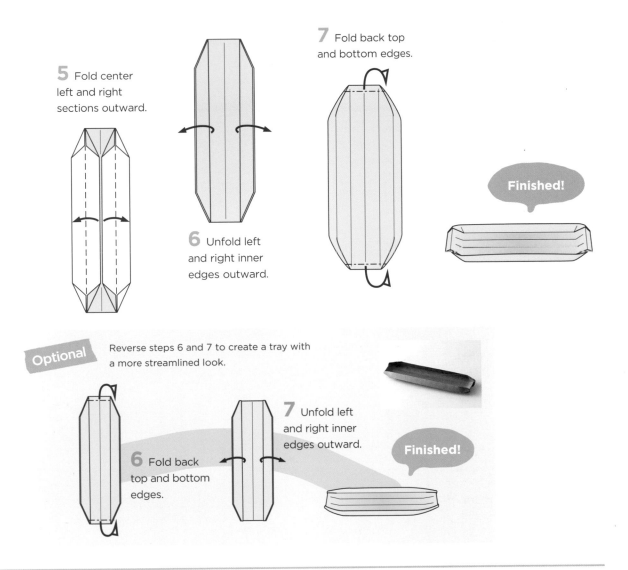

6 Unfold left and right inner edges outward.

7 Fold back top and bottom edges.

Finished!

Optional Reverse steps 6 and 7 to create a tray with a more streamlined look.

6 Fold back top and bottom edges.

7 Unfold left and right inner edges outward.

Finished!

1 Crease along solid line with craft spatula. Fold in left and right edges to the center.

35

30

2 Fold up bottom edge along dashed line. Fold top top edge along dashed line.

8

15

12

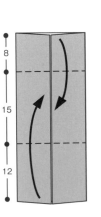

3 Sew on buttons.

5.5

5.5

Finished!

Wrap string around both buttons in a figure 8 to close.

57 Pyramid Potpourri Case (photo pg 108)

What you need : Large Paper: 24 x 24 cm, 2 50-cm strands of string, 2 beads
Small Paper: 18 x 18 cm, 2 40-cm strands of string, 2 beads

Finished size: Large 10 x 10 x 11.5 cm Small 7.5 x 7.5 x 8 cm

Note : Sketch in the lines according to the diagram before folding. Try making this with tracing paper or other translucent material. If you want to add windows, cut them out before you fold.

The numbers in parentheses are for the small size

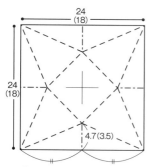

24 (18) 24 (18) 6 (5) 2 (1.5) 4.7(3.5)

1 Sketch in folding lines as indicated. Crease with a craft spatula.

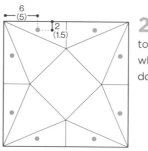

2 Use an awl to create holes where the blue dots are located.

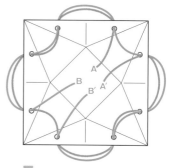

3 Thread one strand of string from A to A'. Thread second string from B to B'.

A A' B B'

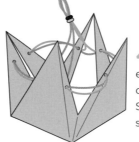

4 Pull up all 4 ends of the strings, creating pyramid. Slide beads onto strings.

Finished!

Optional Add small windows so you can see the potpourri.

Finished!

In step 2, use a utility knife to cut small rectangles in one side.

58 Tissue Case (photo pg 109)

Paper size : 23 x 23 cm

Finished size : 11.5 x 8 cm

Note : The center strips and triangular sections on the finished design show the reverse side of the paper, so be sure to use paper printed on both sides. Use fairly sturdy craft or *washi* paper that'll hold up under frequent use.

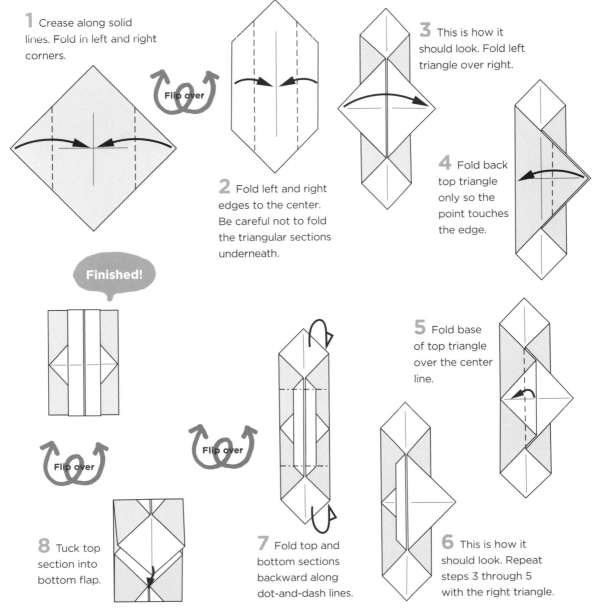

1 Crease along solid lines. Fold in left and right corners.

Flip over

2 Fold left and right edges to the center. Be careful not to fold the triangular sections underneath.

3 This is how it should look. Fold left triangle over right.

4 Fold back top triangle only so the point touches the edge.

5 Fold base of top triangle over the center line.

6 This is how it should look. Repeat steps 3 through 5 with the right triangle.

7 Fold top and bottom sections backward along dot-and-dash lines.

Flip over

8 Tuck top section into bottom flap.

Flip over

Finished!

60 Card Case (photo pg 110)

Paper size : 15 x 15 cm

Finished size : 6 x 9 cm

> **Note :** Fit the paper to the card you want to use. Use paper that's resilient and sturdy.

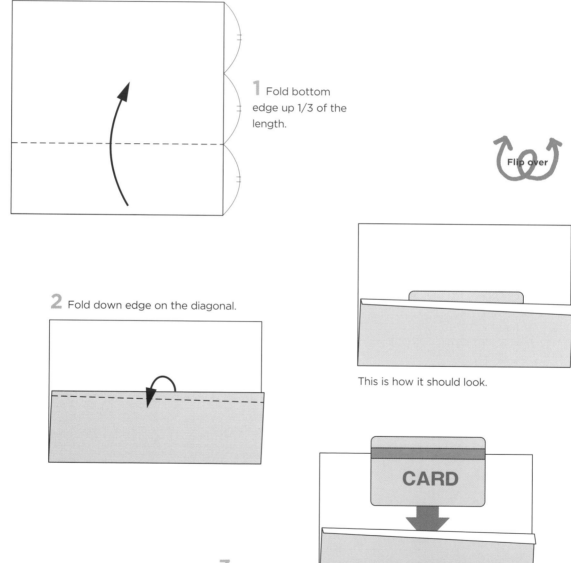

1 Fold bottom edge up 1/3 of the length.

Flip over

2 Fold down edge on the diagonal.

This is how it should look.

CARD

3 Place card in the center.

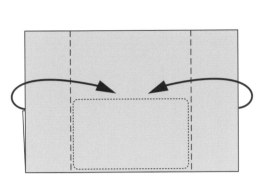

4 Fold left and right sides along card's edges.

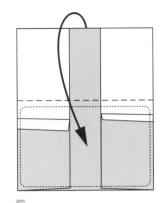

5 Fold top edge down, in line with the top of the card.

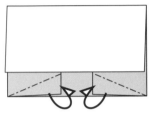

6 Remove card. Mountain fold along dot-and-dash lines and tuck bottom corners underneath.

8 Mountain fold along dot-and-dash lines and tuck corners underneath.

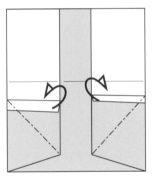

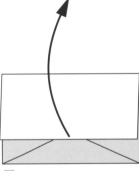

7 Unfold top section.

9 Fold top down, tucking inside triangular folds.

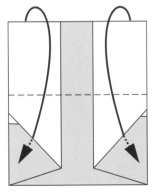

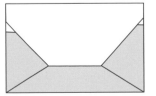

This is how it should look.

Flip over

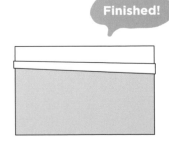

Finished!

60 Folding Card Case (photo pg 111)

Paper size : 30 x 22 cm

Finished size : 9 x 6 cm

> **Note :** Sturdy paper with a fun pattern is best for this case.

1 Fold in half, then unfold.

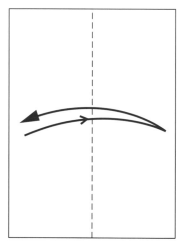

4 Fold edges along creases made in step 2.

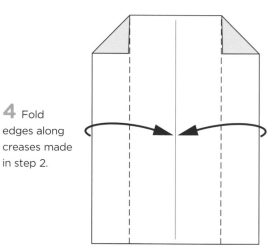

2 Place card you want to use 0.5 cm from the center crease. Fold right edge along card edge, then unfold. Fold left edge in the same manner, then unfold.

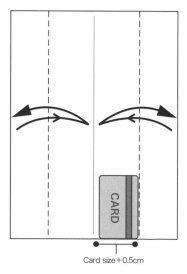

Card size+0.5cm

3 Fold top right and left corners to the creases on the right and left sides.

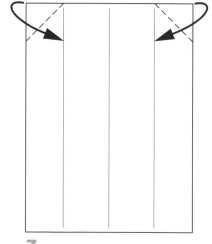

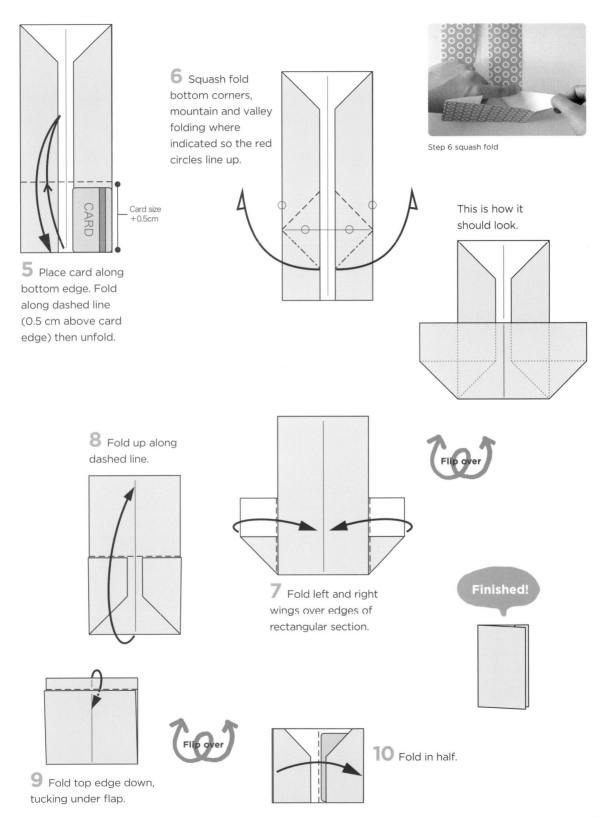

5 Place card along bottom edge. Fold along dashed line (0.5 cm above card edge) then unfold.

CARD

Card size +0.5cm

6 Squash fold bottom corners, mountain and valley folding where indicated so the red circles line up.

Step 6 squash fold

This is how it should look.

8 Fold up along dashed line.

Flip over

7 Fold left and right wings over edges of rectangular section.

Finished!

9 Fold top edge down, tucking under flap.

Flip over

10 Fold in half.

Part 5
Decorations for Every Season

64 **Paper Crane**

The beauty of paper is that it blends so well with whatever decor you already have. Try creating new origami to celebrate each new season.

62 **Plum Blossoms**
Instructions ······ **139**

New Year's flowers.

Elegant paper cranes are often used as New Year's decorations in Japan. Try folding with washi paper for a taste of the East.

The joy of a picturesque springtime.

63 **Butterfly**
Instructions **140**

64 **Mustard Blossoms**
Instructions **139**

Lured by the spring sun, butterflies land on flowers. We used cloth for this background, but try affixing the origami to a sheet of paper or arranging them on a dish.

Paper dolls to celebrate the blossoms on fruit trees.

65 **Dolls**
Instructions ······ **142**

66 **Offering Box**
Instructions ······ **144**

Try making these dolls with finely
textured and prettily matching paper.
Decorate with peach blossoms.

A warrior's helmet for Memorial Day.

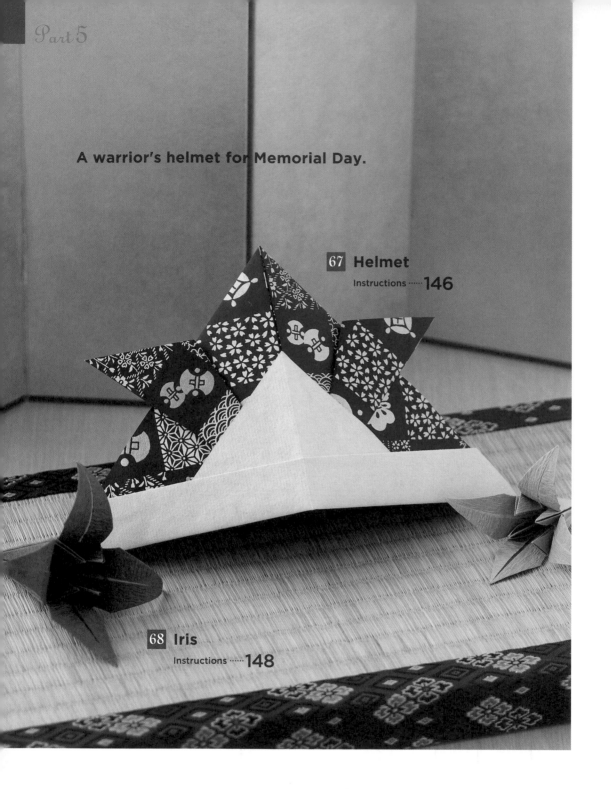

67 **Helmet**
Instructions ······ **146**

68 **Iris**
Instructions ······ **148**

Both of these designs are based on traditional
patterns that create bold, stunning origami.
The irises seem to invite warm summer breezes.

Make these goldfish swim in a cool glass bowl.

69 Goldfish Balloon
Instructions ⋯⋯ **150**

70 Hydrangea
Instructions ⋯⋯ **138**

We arranged these radiant blow-up goldfish with cool hydrangea blossoms. Seeing them in a clear glass bowl makes you almost hear them splashing around.

Autumn brings dragonflies dancing in the evening sunlight. Yellow Evening Primroses complete the autumnal color scheme.

71 Dragonfly

Instructions ······ **152**

72 Evening Primrose

Instructions ······ **139**

Red and orange dragonflies of fall.

A heartwarming wintertime scene

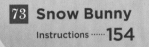

73 **Snow Bunny**
Instructions ······ **154**

74 75 **Camellia and Leaf**
Instructions ······ **155, 156**

Camellias in winter, snow-covered ground and two pale pink bunnies. Soft washi paper gives them a fuzzy, furry look.

61 Paper Crane (photo pg 128)

Paper size : 18 x 18 cm

Finished size : 8 x 13 x 10 cm

Note : Step 12 can be difficult if the paper is very thick. You can skip this step and still make a crane.

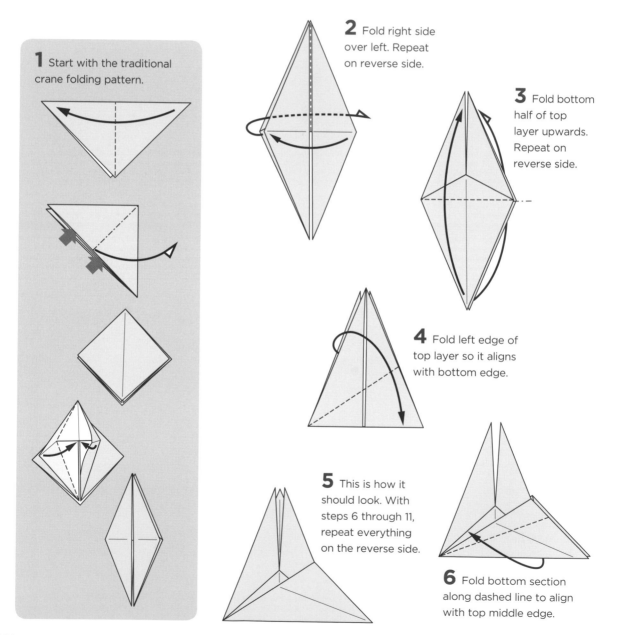

1 Start with the traditional crane folding pattern.

2 Fold right side over left. Repeat on reverse side.

3 Fold bottom half of top layer upwards. Repeat on reverse side.

4 Fold left edge of top layer so it aligns with bottom edge.

5 This is how it should look. With steps 6 through 11, repeat everything on the reverse side.

6 Fold bottom section along dashed line to align with top middle edge.

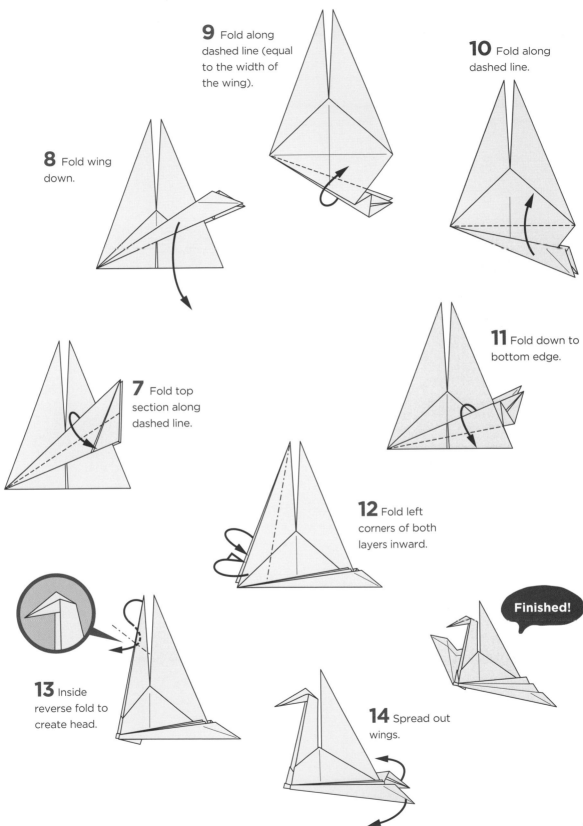

9 Fold along dashed line (equal to the width of the wing).

10 Fold along dashed line.

8 Fold wing down.

7 Fold top section along dashed line.

11 Fold down to bottom edge.

12 Fold left corners of both layers inward.

13 Inside reverse fold to create head.

14 Spread out wings.

Finished!

70 Hydrangea (photo pg 133)

Paper size : 7.5 x 7.5 cm

Finished size : 5 x 3.5 cm

Note : Fold paper in half with the colored side on the inside.

*This is the basic design used for Plum Blossom, Mustard Blossom and Evening Primrose.

1 Start with the same basic squash folds used when making a crane.

Finished!

2

3

Tuck in fingers as far as possible, then squash from above.

7 This is how it should look. Squash fold left and right sides.

4 Fold top left and right corners to the center. Repeat on reverse side.

5 Fold bottom corner to the top corner.

6 Insert fingers where indicated by gray arrows and expand petals.

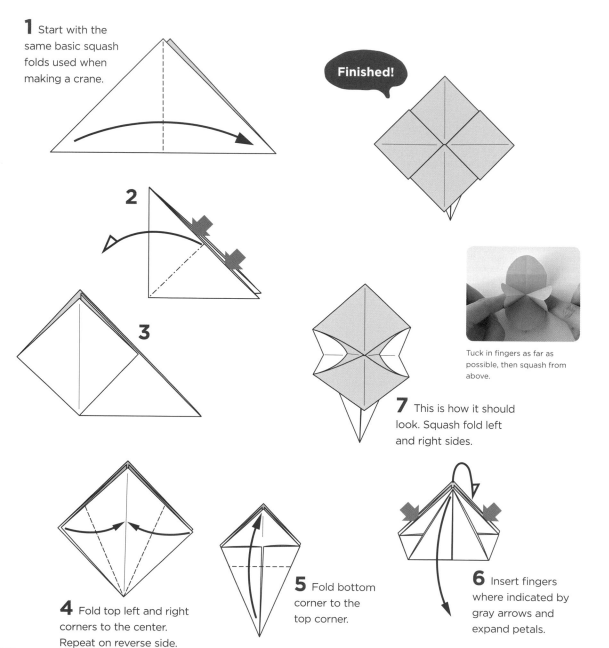

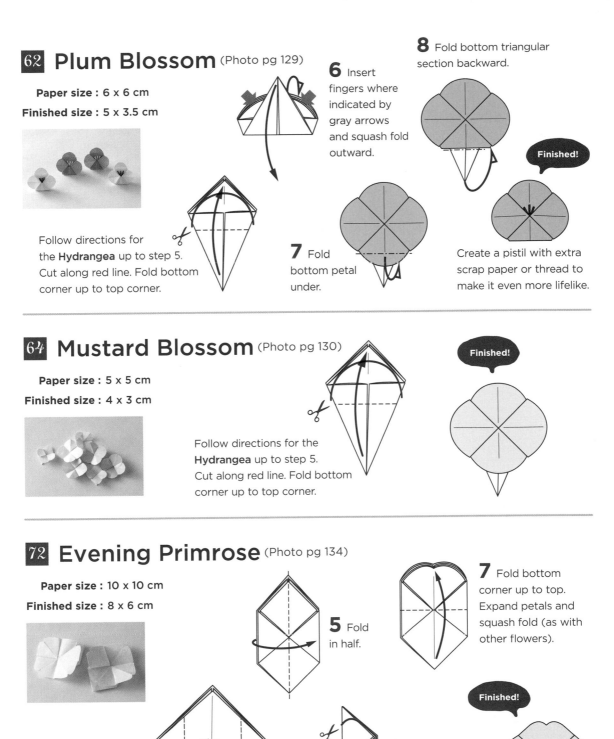

62 **Plum Blossom** (Photo pg 129)

Paper size : 6 x 6 cm
Finished size : 5 x 3.5 cm

Follow directions for the **Hydrangea** up to step 5. Cut along red line. Fold bottom corner up to top corner.

6 Insert fingers where indicated by gray arrows and squash fold outward.

7 Fold bottom petal under.

8 Fold bottom triangular section backward.

Finished!

Create a pistil with extra scrap paper or thread to make it even more lifelike.

64 **Mustard Blossom** (Photo pg 130)

Paper size : 5 x 5 cm
Finished size : 4 x 3 cm

Follow directions for the **Hydrangea** up to step 5. Cut along red line. Fold bottom corner up to top corner.

Finished!

72 **Evening Primrose** (Photo pg 134)

Paper size : 10 x 10 cm
Finished size : 8 x 6 cm

Follow directions for the **Hydrangea** up to step 4. Fold left and right corners to the center. Repeat on reverse side.

5 Fold in half.

6 Cut along red line. Unfold back to step 5.

7 Fold bottom corner up to top. Expand petals and squash fold (as with other flowers).

Finished!

63 **Butterfly** (photo pg 130)

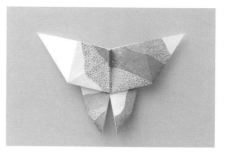

Paper size : Large 15 x 15 cm Small 10 x 10 cm

Finished size : Large 13.5 x 8 cm Small 8.5 x 6 cm

Note : If you choose a patterned paper, keep in mind the folds will affect how the pattern appears.

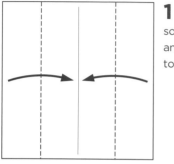

1 Crease along solid line. Fold left and right edges to the center.

2 Fold along dashed line, then unfold.

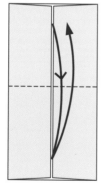

3 Fold bottom and top edges to the center.

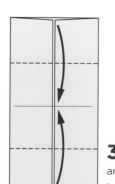

4 Fold top left and right edges to their opposite corners, then unfold.

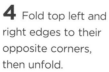

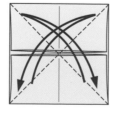

5 Unfold back to step 3. Mountain and valley fold where indicated, lifting up bottom corners.

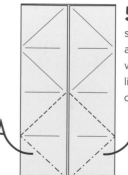

6 Repeat with top corners.

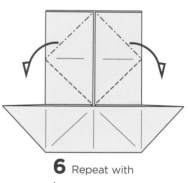

This is how it should look.

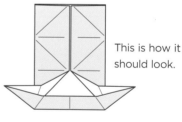

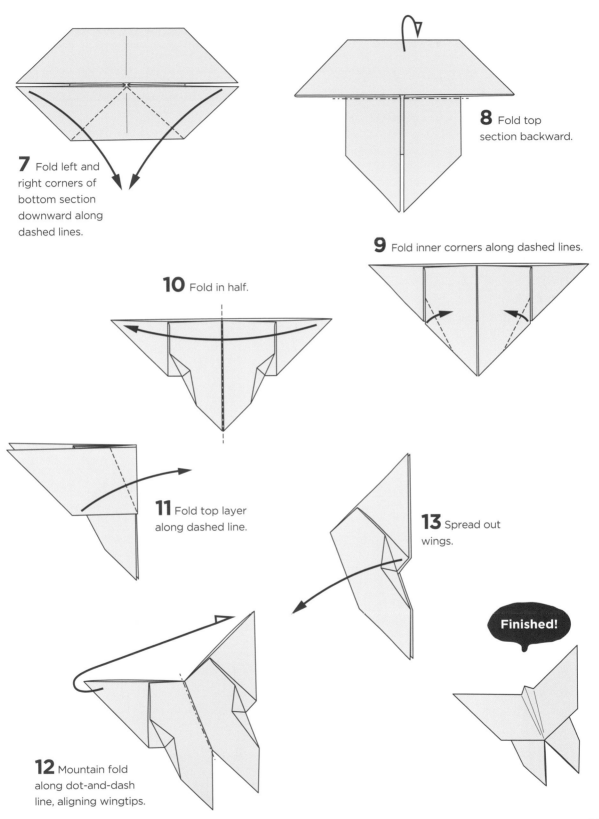

7 Fold left and right corners of bottom section downward along dashed lines.

8 Fold top section backward.

9 Fold inner corners along dashed lines.

10 Fold in half.

11 Fold top layer along dashed line.

12 Mountain fold along dot-and-dash line, aligning wingtips.

13 Spread out wings.

Finished!

141

65 Dolls (photo pg 131)

Paper size : 20 x 20 cm

Finished size : 7.5 x 8.5 cm

Note : The boy doll and girl doll are folded the same way up to step 6. If you want to make the white part stand out, affix thicker craft or calligraphy paper before folding.

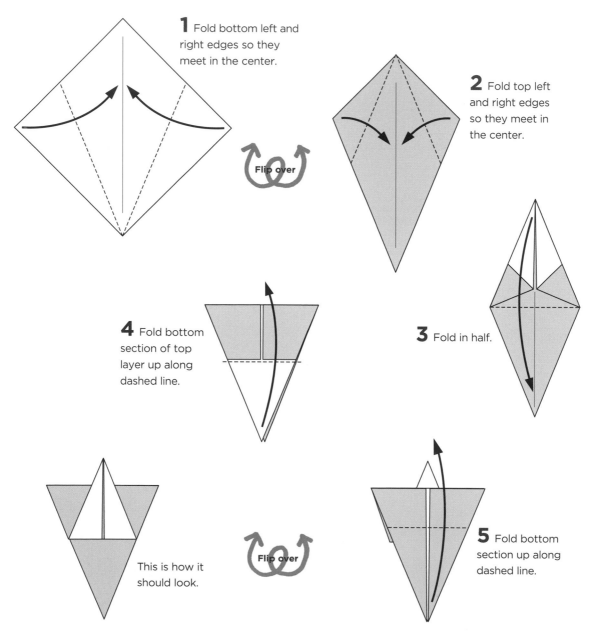

1 Fold bottom left and right edges so they meet in the center.

Flip over

2 Fold top left and right edges so they meet in the center.

3 Fold in half.

4 Fold bottom section of top layer up along dashed line.

5 Fold bottom section up along dashed line.

This is how it should look.

Flip over

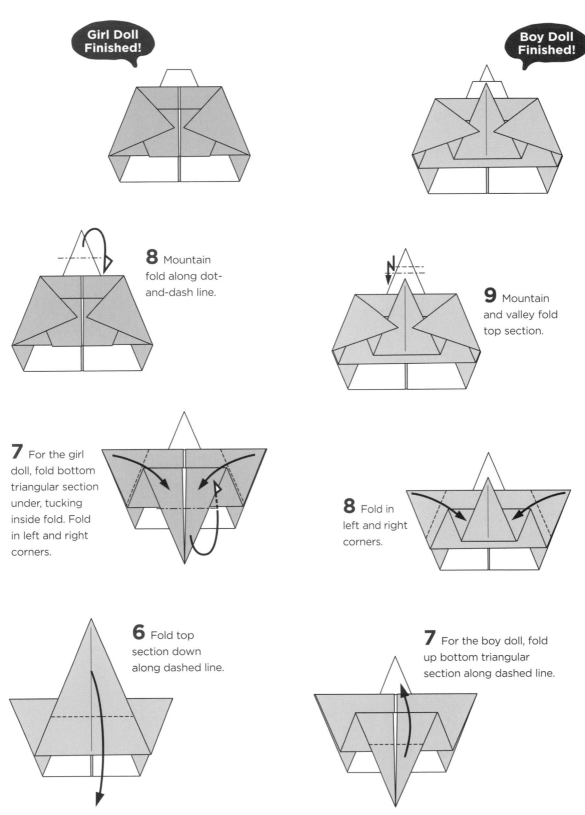

Girl Doll Finished!

Boy Doll Finished!

8 Mountain fold along dot-and-dash line.

9 Mountain and valley fold top section.

7 For the girl doll, fold bottom triangular section under, tucking inside fold. Fold in left and right corners.

8 Fold in left and right corners.

6 Fold top section down along dashed line.

7 For the boy doll, fold up bottom triangular section along dashed line.

143

66 Offering Box (photo pg 131)

Paper size : 12 x 12 cm

Finished size : 9 x 3 x 3 cm

Note : If you want to make a larger version, use sturdy paper or two sheets glued together.

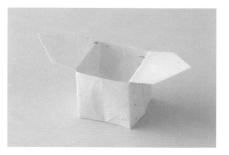

1 Crease along solid lines.
Fold each corner to the center.

2 Mountain fold along dot-and-dash line.

3 Fold in half.

4 Squash fold top layer to the right.

5 Repeat on reverse side.

This is how it should look.

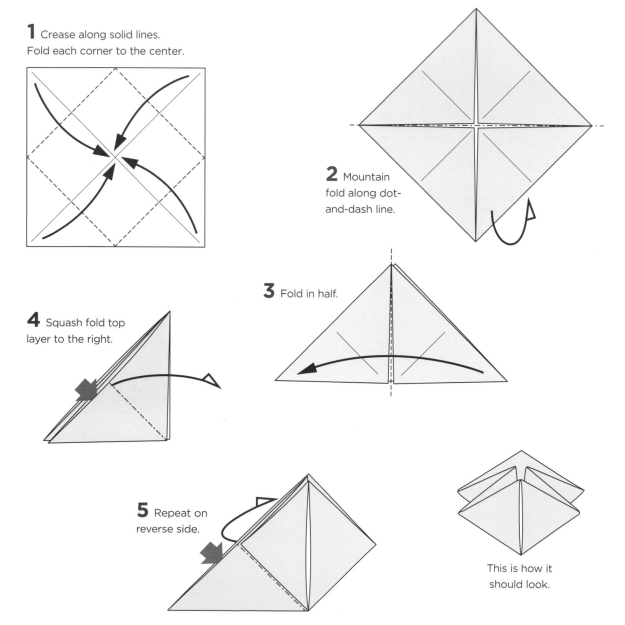

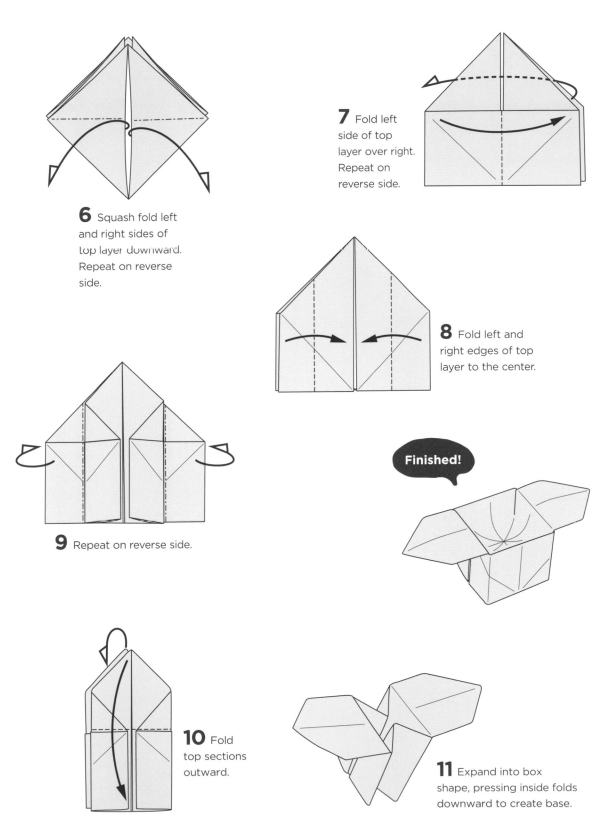

6 Squash fold left and right sides of top layer downward. Repeat on reverse side.

7 Fold left side of top layer over right. Repeat on reverse side.

8 Fold left and right edges of top layer to the center.

9 Repeat on reverse side.

Finished!

10 Fold top sections outward.

11 Expand into box shape, pressing inside folds downward to create base.

67 Helmet (photo pg 132)

Paper size : 34 x 34 cm

Finished size : 12 x 24 cm

> **Note :** Traditionally, the final flap is folded backwards, but we want this to look good from any angle, so we'll fold it under instead.

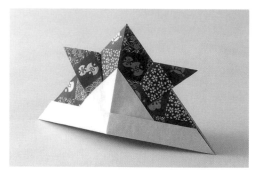

1 Fold in half.

Turn 180°

3 Fold bottom corners to the top.

2 Fold in half, then unfold.

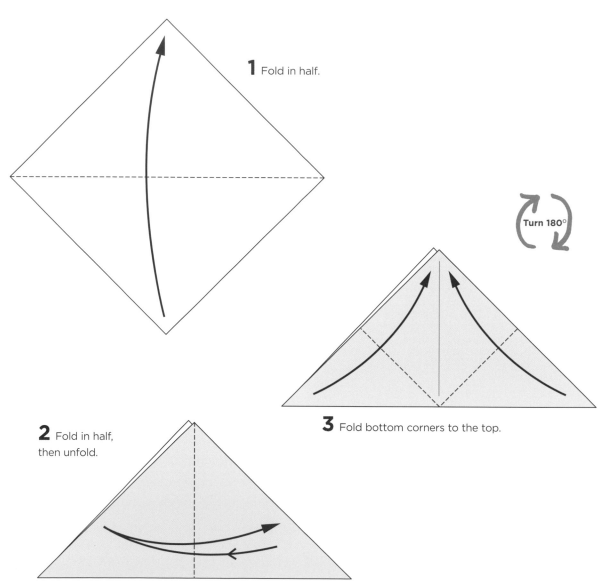

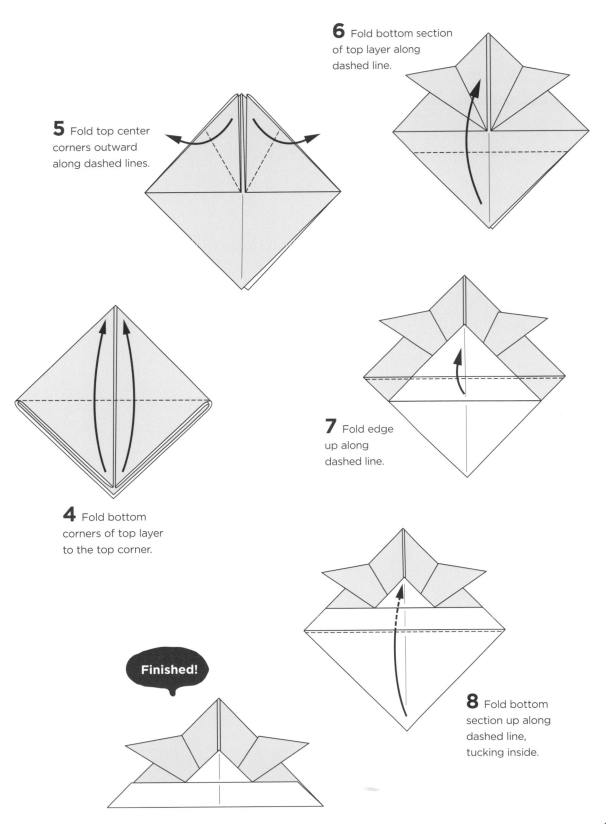

5 Fold top center corners outward along dashed lines.

6 Fold bottom section of top layer along dashed line.

4 Fold bottom corners of top layer to the top corner.

7 Fold edge up along dashed line.

Finished!

8 Fold bottom section up along dashed line, tucking inside.

68 Iris (photo pg 132)

Paper size : 16 x 16 cm

Finished size : 8 x 8 x 10 cm

> **Note :** There are many fine folds, but don't let it stress you out. The reverse side of the paper peeks out, giving an elegant feel.

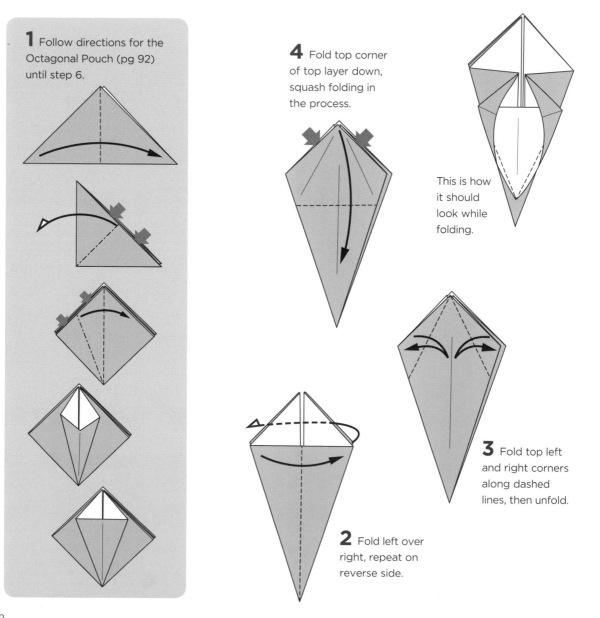

1 Follow directions for the Octagonal Pouch (pg 92) until step 6.

2 Fold left over right, repeat on reverse side.

3 Fold top left and right corners along dashed lines, then unfold.

4 Fold top corner of top layer down, squash folding in the process.

This is how it should look while folding.

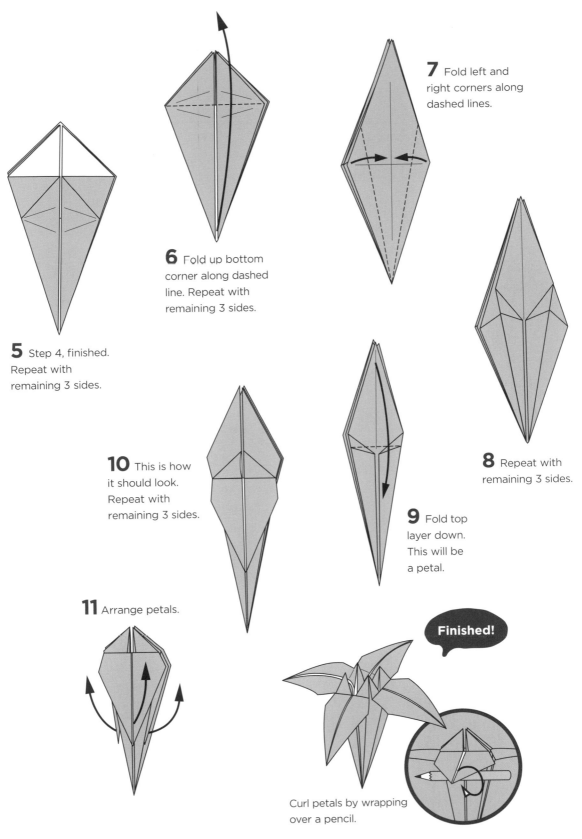

5 Step 4, finished. Repeat with remaining 3 sides.

6 Fold up bottom corner along dashed line. Repeat with remaining 3 sides.

7 Fold left and right corners along dashed lines.

8 Repeat with remaining 3 sides.

9 Fold top layer down. This will be a petal.

10 This is how it should look. Repeat with remaining 3 sides.

11 Arrange petals.

Finished!

Curl petals by wrapping over a pencil.

69 Goldfish Balloon (photo pg 133)

Paper size : Large 15 x 15 cm Small 10 x 10 cm

Finished size : Large 4 x 10.5 x 7 cm Small 2.5 x 7 x 4 cm

Note : This is based on the traditional balloon design.

1 Fold in half.

2 Fold in half.

3 Lift up and squash fold top layer to the right.

4 This is how it should look. Repeat on reverse side.

5 Fold left and right corners to the top.

6 Fold top left and right corners to the center.

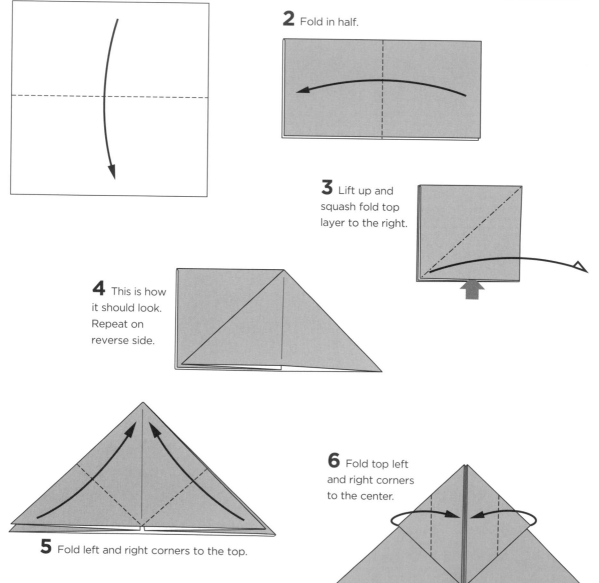

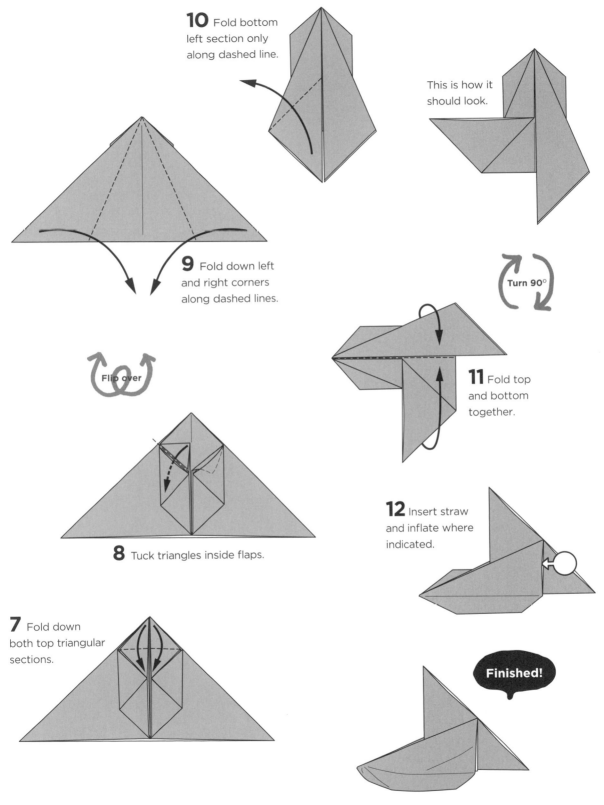

10 Fold bottom left section only along dashed line.

This is how it should look.

9 Fold down left and right corners along dashed lines.

Turn 90°

Flip over

11 Fold top and bottom together.

8 Tuck triangles inside flaps.

12 Insert straw and inflate where indicated.

7 Fold down both top triangular sections.

Finished!

71 Dragonfly (photo pg 134)

Paper size : Large 15 x 15 cm   Small 12 x 12 cm

Finished size : Large 12 x 10 x 2 cm   Small 10 x 8 x 2 cm

Note : This is a variation on the traditional crane design. Let's appreciate its age-old artistry.

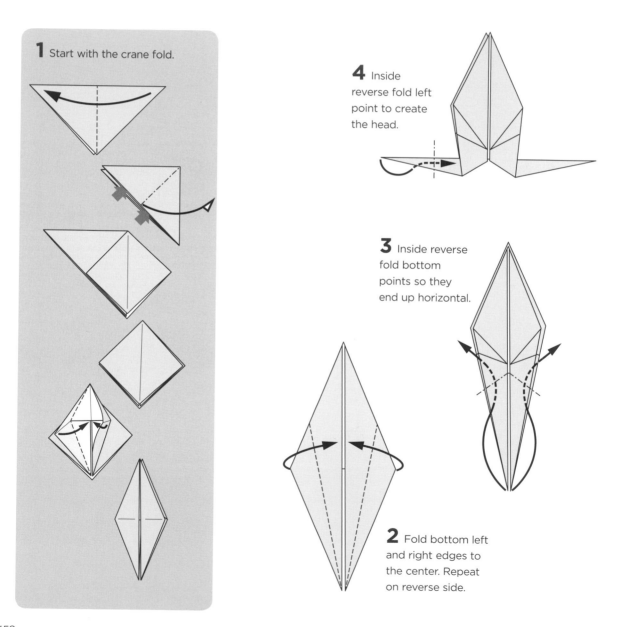

1 Start with the crane fold.

4 Inside reverse fold left point to create the head.

3 Inside reverse fold bottom points so they end up horizontal.

2 Fold bottom left and right edges to the center. Repeat on reverse side.

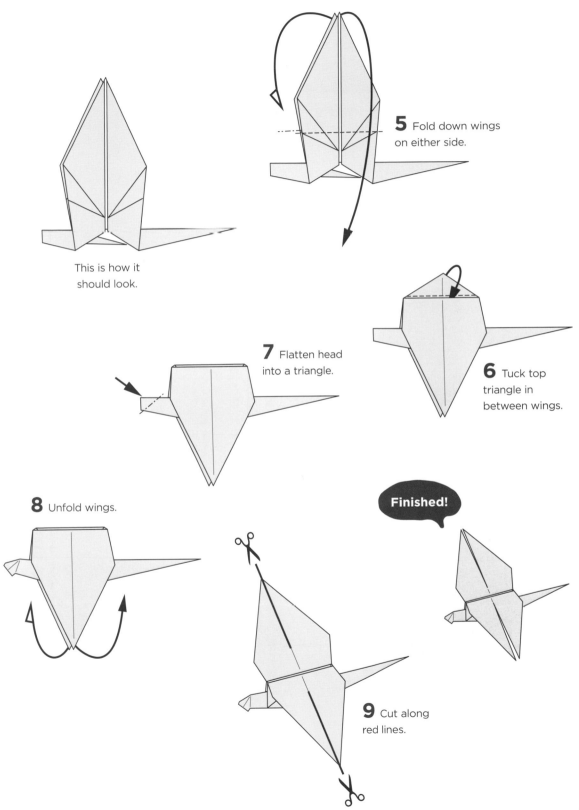

This is how it should look.

5 Fold down wings on either side.

6 Tuck top triangle in between wings.

7 Flatten head into a triangle.

8 Unfold wings.

Finished!

9 Cut along red lines.

73 Snow Bunny (photo pg 135)

Paper size : 18 x 18 cm

Finished size : 5.5 x 6 x 6.5 cm

Note : Try using paper with different colors on each side. This is based on the traditional balloon design.

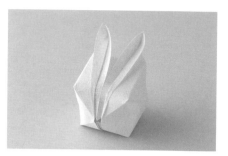

1 With colored side facing you, follow directions for Goldfish Balloon (pg 150) to step 5.

4 Mountain fold along dot-and-dash lines.

Flip over

This is how it should look.

2 Fold left and right corners to the center.

3 Fold top corners in order along dashed lines, tucking into flaps.

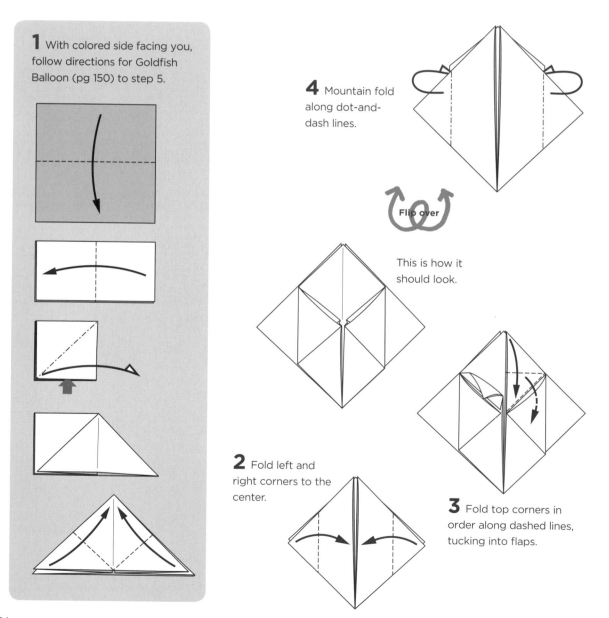

5 Fold top center sections along dashed lines.

6 Open where indicated by arrows to create ears. Blow into center opening to inflate.

Finished!

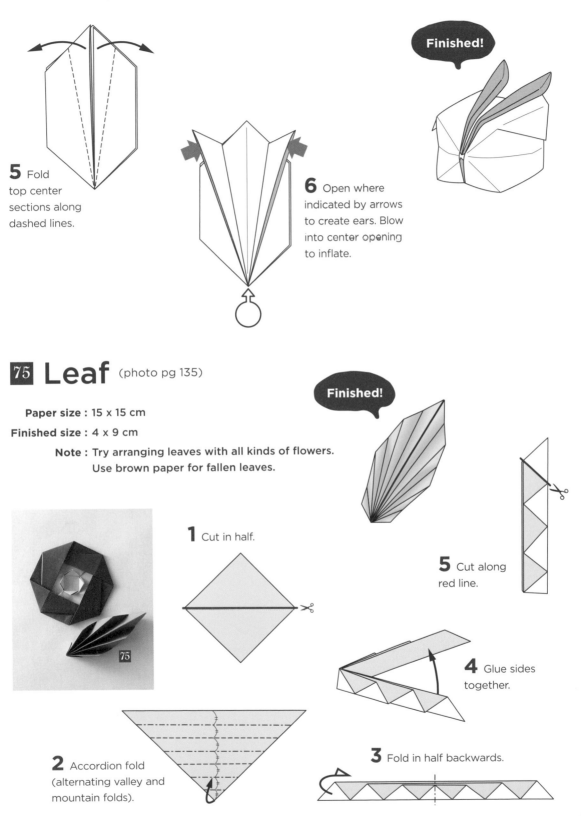

75 Leaf (photo pg 135)

Paper size : 15 x 15 cm

Finished size : 4 x 9 cm

Note : Try arranging leaves with all kinds of flowers. Use brown paper for fallen leaves.

Finished!

1 Cut in half.

5 Cut along red line.

4 Glue sides together.

3 Fold in half backwards.

2 Accordion fold (alternating valley and mountain folds).

74 Camellia (photo pg 135)

Paper size : 15 x 15 cm

Finished size : 8 cm diameter

Note : This uses the same kimono-folding technique used for the pouches. Take your time and make sure of each step before continuing.

1 Crease along solid lines. Fold up bottom edge so the circles align.

6 Fold top left corner so circles align.

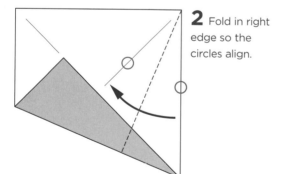

2 Fold in right edge so the circles align.

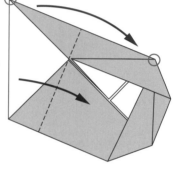

5 Squash fold top right corner to the left.

3 Squash fold bottom right corner up.

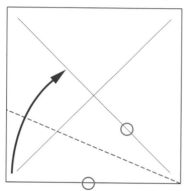

4 Fold top edge down so circles align.

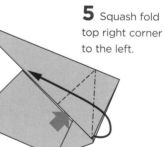

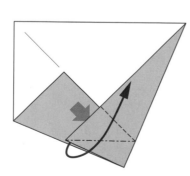

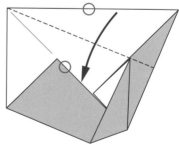

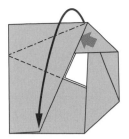

7 Squash fold top corner to the bottom.

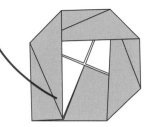

8 Unfold left triangle to the left, returning to step 6.

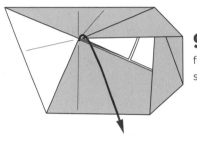

9 Lift up and fold bottom section outward.

10 A→B

Edge A folded over. Pick up to left corner.

10 B

Insert top left corner under bottom flap.

10 B→C

Point B folded down. Fold bottom layer back over.

Ⓐ

10 This is how it should look. Ⓐ Fold in at crease on right. Ⓑ Pinch corner with star into bottom flap. Ⓒ Fold corner from step 9 back over to original position.

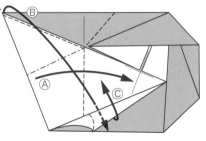

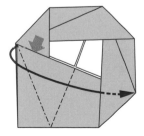

11 Squash fold left corner to the right, tucking in.

12 Fold inner corners outward along dashed lines.

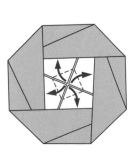

Finished!

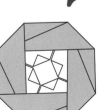

157

Cute Craft

Aranzi Aronzo have a whole line of whimsical, adorable and easy-to-make crafts. Get started with *Cute Stuff* and catch the crafting bug!

Cute Stuff
$14.95/$16.95